Praise for Denise Duffield-Thomas

"Denise has helped her growing community of
120,000+ business owners overcome their money
blocks and build successful companies."
FORBES.COM

"Denise is one of the most honest, transparent,
unapologetic voices out there leading women
to prosperity. Her work is so important."
KATE NORTHRUP, AUTHOR OF *MONEY, A LOVE STORY*

"Denise offers ... so much value and openly
and honestly shares what has worked well
for her business – and what has not."
THE HUFFINGTON POST

"I am a massive fan of Denise, her books, and her
courses. Down to earth, honest, and at times hilarious,
DDT shows us how to create a truly exceptional life."
REBECCA CAMPBELL, AUTHOR OF *LIGHT IS THE NEW BLACK* AND *RISE SISTER RISE*

"Denise Duffield-Thomas [is] one of the
foremost financial advisors for females."
ENTREPRENEUR.COM

"Denise is one of the world's best teacher on the Law
of Attraction. Every day she impresses me with her
wisdom, business savvy, integrity, and teachings."
LEONIE DAWSON, AUTHOR OF *LESSONS EVERY GODDESS MUST
KNOW* AND THE *SHINING YEAR* WORKBOOKS

"Denise is the ultimate money mindset mentor. With
her systems, tools, and tricks to open up your heart and
mind to receive the abundance that is your birthright, you
can't fail. Everybody needs some Denise in their life."
SUSIE MOORE, AUTHOR OF *WHAT IF IT DOES WORK OUT?*

"Denise is a refreshing voice on money mindset. She writes in a way that is easeful and humorous, and you'll feel like she's right there with you as you put her lessons to work and create a more abundant business and life."

Also by Denise Duffield-Thomas

Lucky Bitch

Get Rich, Lucky Bitch!

Also by Denise Duffield-Thomas

Lucky Bitch

Get Rich, Lucky Bitch!

Release Your
Money Blocks and
Live a First-Class Life

DENISE DUFFIELD-THOMAS

HAY HOUSE

Carlsbad, California • New York City
London • Sydney • New Delhi

Published in the United Kingdom by:
Hay House UK Ltd, Astley House, 33 Notting Hill Gate, London W11 3JQ
Tel: +44 (0)20 3675 2450; Fax: +44 (0)20 3675 2451; www.hayhouse.co.uk

Published in the United States of America by:
Hay House Inc., PO Box 5100, Carlsbad, CA 92018-5100
Tel: (1) 760 431 7695 or (800) 654 5126; Fax: (1) 760 431 6948 or (800) 650 5115
www.hayhouse.com

Published in Australia by:
Hay House Australia Ltd, 18/36 Ralph St, Alexandria NSW 2015
Tel: (61) 2 9669 4299; Fax: (61) 2 9669 4144; www.hayhouse.com.au

Published in India by:
Hay House Publishers India, Muskaan Complex, Plot No.3, B-2,
Vasant Kunj, New Delhi 110 070
Tel: (91) 11 4176 1620; Fax: (91) 11 4176 1630; www.hayhouse.co.in

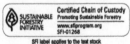

*This book is dedicated to you.
Daring to live a richer life will give other women
permission to do the same, and together,
we're going to change the world.*

Contents

Contents

Introduction

"Money makes the world go around."

EMCEE, CABARET

*H*ey, Lucky Bee!

Today is the start of your richer life – one of outrageous material and spiritual abundance (these aren't mutually exclusive, by the way). And it's the start of effortlessly creating your First-Class life. I'm thrilled that you're joining me on this journey. Because, yes, your path to riches really is a fascinating journey, and I know you picked up this book because you're ready. It's your time and you're ready for the next step.

Pretty much my whole life, I've dreamed of having enough money to do everything on my vision board; and since you're reading this book, I'm guessing that one of your dreams is to be wealthy too. Money *does* make the world go round. However, unfortunately, many women aren't getting rich – because they think that being rich means being a bitch (or snobby, or ruthless, etc.)

Collectively, as a gender, we've got all these funky self-beliefs and fears about money, so I wrote this book to give *you* permission to be as rich as you want. There's no amount of money you could want that's too big or too small. You can seriously have all the abundance you want if you follow the predictable laws of the Universe. There are no exceptions. You don't have to "deserve" it. It's yours if you want it.

Want to be a Serious Business Lady – swanning around the world on your personalized private jet, like a *boss*? Done.

Want to be a millionaire? Do it.

What about just having extra money to hire a cleaner once a week, take another holiday each year, or buy a new car? Consider it yours.

Helping women to get out of their own way and overcome their money blocks is now my favorite hobby, as well as my life's work. And trust me: no matter where you're starting from, if you're willing to uncover what's holding *you* back, you *will* create money miracles in your life.

In return, I promise that I'll be straight with you about what it *really* takes to uncover your true wealth and manifest money. I've been told many times that I have a knack for making complicated things seem really easy. That's because I'm honest – and frankly, I can't be bothered to BS you. I'll tell you what works and what doesn't.

For many women, being rich seems like a fantasy: one that's *juuust* out of reach, or only for other women – the ones who have their acts together. You know, women with perfect thighs, the perfect husband, or the perfect childhood. (Spoiler alert: I have none of these things, although my husband *is* pretty awesome.)

Women tell me they won't ever be rich because, deep down, they're afraid that it would turn them into a bitch, or that their friends and family wouldn't like them anymore. *That* self-limiting belief is just as damaging for getting wealthy as thinking you have to be perfect first.

However, if you have the self-awareness, and you're willing to admit that only *you* are holding yourself back from being rich... well, that's a great start, and you already have everything you need to become as rich as you want.

When I ask clients and women in my seminars to tell me why they don't make as much money as they want, this is what I hear:

+ I'm just no good with money.

+ I've reached the limit of my earning potential.

+ I'm doing great: it would be greedy to want more.

+ I should be earning more, but I'm afraid it will cost too much (in terms of health or relationships).

+ My partner takes care of our money.

+ I'm just afraid to even look at my finances.

+ I wish I could just win the lottery.

+ Money just isn't that important to me.

+ I have a good life, and I should just be happy with that.

+ I'm smart, but I just can't seem to break through to the next level.

It actually doesn't matter *why* you believe you don't earn enough, because whatever you come up with is just a story you're telling yourself. It's not really true, and it also doesn't have to be that way anymore.

I freely admit that *I* used to have a bad relationship with money. I was terrified of fully expressing my potential, and I worried what my friends and family would think about me being rich. I sabotaged myself and my career, even though I knew that I was smart and capable. I couldn't make any money from my various businesses, even though I knew that I was a born entrepreneur.

I practically *repelled* money! But not anymore.

Now, yes, I have an amazing and abundant life. (It would be weird to write a book about money if I hadn't figured it out, right?) I travel whenever I like and rarely stress about money like I used to. I have world-class mentors and a great support team, and I live in my dream house. But I'm still just a regular person. I'm still me, and I'm far from perfect. (For some reason, I used to think I'd have to change *everything* about myself to be "worthy" of success.)

In full disclosure, I wrote the first edition of this book when I hadn't yet reached the million-dollar mark, although my business was successful. And at the time, part of me was like, "Who am I to write this?"

Becoming a millionaire *still* didn't change who I was – I'm still imperfect, and that's okay. There are many things left in my life to upgrade, but I know that it doesn't always happen overnight. This is a lifelong journey for *all* of us.

Now I set *big* money goals, and I achieve them. Not out of fear and panic, but just as a game; and I constantly work on myself so I can go to the next level. It's actually *fun* to make money now, and it's fun to spend it without second-guessing myself.

Plus, I'm *finally* surrounded by strong, powerful women who also make shitloads of money by creating good in the world. I don't have clothes with holes in them anymore. I don't walk in the rain because I can't afford a cab anymore, and I'm not cheap with myself anymore.

Guess what? I'm no smarter than I was before. I'm no prettier, skinnier, or even "luckier." I just put all my effort into overcoming my money "stuff" (using all the tips that I'll share in this book), and the rest fell into place more easily than I would have thought possible.

So, now I spend my time analyzing exactly what works and what doesn't, in order to manifest my ideal life. I've now taught tens of thousands of women all around the world how to use the Law of Attraction in an incredibly practical and real way that *actually works*.

I'm not talking about airy-fairy concepts like "abundance" here. I'm saying that you can have more money in your pocket, feel richer on a daily basis, and have a kick-ass life. Yes, *you!*

I wrote this book after I created my popular online Money Bootcamp. After the first hundred women had completed the lessons, I knew we were onto something really special – because the results they achieved were incredible. Most of the women changed their mindset *forever*, and others made huge inroads every day. Word started to spread until we had five hundred students, then a thousand, then two thousand... then we doubled that, and keep growing every day.

I started to get emails every day from women asking when I was running the next Bootcamp. At first, I planned to run the course just a few times a year; however, demand was so high, I decided to open it up so women could join anytime. Money blocks wait for nobody!

But I knew that not everyone could afford the tuition to change their money mindset (ironic, right?!). So I wanted to create an affordable option for women to learn the concepts I teach about becoming wealthy. Hence the book in your hands! As you implement all the abundance tips I share in it, you *will* become richer – and you'll probably realize exactly why you've been holding yourself back for so long.

Important: Don't discount this book if you're already doing well financially. You've probably done a lot of personal development and already have an abundance mindset. But I find that women who are successful are always looking for new improvements and tweaks, so they can create even more abundance and satisfaction in their lives.

That's why I know you'll get tons out of this book too. No matter how much money you earn, chances are that you'll reach another income ceiling. When that happens, you can take everything much deeper and ask: *What else can I learn about myself?* And of course, if you're ready for more support and an incredible group experience with other awesome women, check out www.DeniseDT.com/Bootcamp for information on how to join our unique community.

The truth is that the path to creating your rich life can sometimes be a lonely one. Maybe you're the black sheep in your family (like I am), or the only person creating success in your circle of friends. Or maybe you're surrounded by rich dudes and want some like-minded sisters to network and mastermind with? Whichever's true for you, you're in the right place.

The Lucky Bee (we don't call each other bitches) community is a powerful one that spans the globe, and now you're a part of it. Welcome! Together, our power is multiplied, so never feel like you're alone on this journey. Together we're growing every day. This is a safe place to brag about your successes (financial or otherwise) and share honestly about your fears. Now is the time for us as women to rise up and get rich; and I'm having so much fun being a part of it. Together, we're changing the world!

Let me tell you how this all started

In my first book, *Lucky Bitch*, I shared my secrets to becoming extraordinarily lucky, and deconstructed exactly how to make the Law of Attraction work for you in the real world. That book has now been read by women in more than 160 countries around the world – I get emails every day from them, describing the stories of their magic, hustle, and luck.

Lucky Bitch tells the story of how I became an unbelievable manifestor. In the space of one year, applying my secret Manifesting Formula (which isn't really secret at all: it's more like a mix of practical actions and metaphysical techniques), I became this crazy-lucky person. Hence the name *Lucky Bitch*. Everything I put on my dream board came true. I just kept winning stuff. Honestly, it was unbelievable: I felt like I was in a movie.

It started with little things, like winning small amounts of money at bingo. (I love bingo... now. I used to get really nervous playing it though, and I *never* won.) After that, I was given a ticket to a seminar in Las Vegas ($1,500 value) that I'd desperately wanted to attend, then a free space on a weight-loss course I thought would be life-changing for me ($200 value).

Then, after setting a goal to work for myself, I just "happened" to win a scholarship for a life coaching qualification, which was worth over $5,000. Then I wanted to write a book, and by "chance," I won a self-publishing home study program in a lucky door prize (over $5,000 value). All of these things were on my goal list, all of them free. I didn't even become a consistent competition enterer – I just entered, and won.

Then I experienced the most amazing manifestation ever. After setting a goal to go traveling for six months, my husband and I won a travel competition with a honeymoon company. The prize was traveling the world for six months, and staying in luxurious resorts and hotels for free. Yes, you read that right: completely free, and with a value of over half a million dollars.

I never thought those things happened in real life, and certainly not to *me*. We quit our jobs, and for six months, explored twelve countries and stayed in the most unbelievable places in the world. We went to New York, Kenya, Mauritius, Zanzibar, Malta, Spain, Jordan, Indonesia, Thailand, the United Kingdom, Ireland, and lastly, Queensland in my home country, Australia.

That trip changed my life. The thing is, we didn't just win the trip: we *consciously manifested* it. We sent constant and specific messages to the Universe that we were ready, willing, and able to leave our crappy apartment in London, throw in our jobs, and take off around the world. I asked the Universe for a life-changing experience, and the Universe delivered! I followed my Manifesting Formula and amazing things happened. Go read *Lucky Bitch* for the whole story.

But the most interesting thing happened *after* the trip ended; and here's where my true abundance journey started. When the travel and free accommodations ended, we didn't even have a place to live anymore. My hubby was in London, tying up loose ends with his career, and I was sleeping on my mother's couch in Australia, jobless and scared. I realized that even after becoming incredibly lucky, *I was still broke.* I could manifest half a million dollars' worth of free stuff, but I'd never earned more than a small salary in "real money." Lucky, yes; but *wealthy?* Nope.

I remember a few people had said to me during the all-expenses paid trip: "Well, what are you going to do when you have to go back to the *real* world?" I basically wanted to tell them to f-off. I knew that I *was* living in the real world – because I'd had a glimpse of what life was really like for some people.

I saw how rich people vacationed. I saw how nice life could be with money, but I still had massive resistance to earning it myself. And, to be honest, the idea of money scared the crap out of me. Even though, *intellectually*, I wanted to be rich.

After the trip ended and I started out as a fledging life coach, I remember sweating with anxiety the first time I met with an accountant about my new business. I felt like I was going to get into trouble. I was crapping myself about paying taxes before I earned my first thousand bucks. On top of that, after living in five-star hotels for six months, my husband and I had moved into a small apartment that was pretty similar to our old one, in spite of being in a completely different country.

The result of all that was that when I started teaching people everything I knew about the Law of Attraction, even though I knew I had a gift, I didn't feel worthy of being a success teacher. To be honest, I felt like the biggest fraud ever.

I surveyed my blog subscribers at that time to ask them about *their* biggest goals and biggest obstacles. At least 80 percent of the responses mentioned *money*. People told me their fears around money: mostly that they would never have enough or would never earn what they felt they were worth.

They spoke about their desire to live up to the potential they knew was inside them. They told me how blocked they felt, and how they lay awake at night wishing things were different. Yup – I knew *exactly* what that felt like too.

My readers told me how they felt like frauds when discussing money with their own clients. They told me their dreams and what they could accomplish if only they could get this "money stuff" under control. They wanted to be rich!

My first reaction was pure panic. *Shiiiiiit. Not money... anything else but that!*

My next thought was: *Well, they'll have to go to someone else.*

The Universe was asking me to step up to fill this role, and I was extremely reluctant – even though I knew it was a lesson I needed to learn. How could I teach something that I was terrible at myself? I ignored the calling for as long as possible. "Not me, Universe. Please. Don't make me do this."

But you're reading this book, so I obviously took on the challenge. (Otherwise, this would be a crap book, right?) It turned out to be an *even greater* adventure than the all-expenses paid trip too (and ultimately, a lot more satisfying).

I spent the next year applying everything I taught about the Law of Attraction; but this time, I applied it *directly* to my money mindset. I dealt with my fear of having money and uncovered every single money memory that was holding me back.

I worked on my negative money beliefs and dug way deep down to find out why I was really scared of being rich. I examined every decision I'd ever made about money, and shone a light on all my mistakes. It was yucky, scary work at times, but oh-so-worth-it, as you'll realize for yourself.

And as a result of all this work, my income doubled, then tripled. I upgraded everything in my life – slowly at first, and then I gained momentum. I had a few setbacks (which you'll experience too, no doubt), and each time, I went straight back to the simple lessons. And seriously, you'll see how simple it is for you too.

Because of this consistent money mindset work, my income grows every single day. Far from being a fluke, the mindset work is an easy and predictable process that anyone can learn, *if* they're willing to do the self-examination. Which, honestly, not everyone *is* willing to do.

But I know you're different.

I now teach the same principles all around the world in my speeches, in my weekly blog posts, and for my private community in my Money Bootcamp. And now, gorgeous, you'll learn them too!

I'm on a mission to change the world through helping women to become rich, because I believe:

❖ Every woman deserves to be as rich as she wants.

❖ Every woman deserves to feel safe and taken care of.

- Every woman deserves to be treated like a VIP.
- Every woman deserves a First-Class life.
- Rich women change the world.

In *Get Rich, Lucky Bitch*, you'll get the tools and inspiration you need to go to the next level of wealth. It doesn't matter if you're starting from scratch or itching to break through the million-dollar mark: you'll realize that the only thing that's stopping you is your past and current beliefs around money. And these can be changed relatively easily when you know how. (Remember: I'm not going to BS you – it takes some work... but it's worth it!)

I've inspired thousands of women around the world to dream bigger and, most importantly, to do the practical work to manifest their dreams in the real world. You won't ever hear me say that you need to *dream harder*.

In fact, I'm probably the most practical manifestation teacher you'll ever meet. You'll get day-to-day actions, inspiration, kick-up-the-butt real talk, and the most loving advice I can give. Because I want you to be rich. Again, why *not* you?

I want us to meet up in Hawaii, or mastermind over cocktails in Vegas. I want us to go on charity trips together to present ridiculous, novelty-sized checks to people who are changing the world on the ground. I want us to go shopping together and buy things that make us feel like a million bucks. How cool would it be to say, "Anyone up for a mastermind weekend with Richard Branson on Necker Island?" and have it just be an easy decision?

When you read books like this, it's easy to imagine the author as different to you. I've done it myself. *Well, it's okay* for **her**. *Of course she has her shiz together, she wrote a* **book** *about it!* But I'm just a normal person. I'm not going to tell you that I've "cracked the code" or make you feel dumb if you don't get it.

Think of me as your sometimes bossy – but usually 100 percent right – Virgo girlfriend and mentor (everyone has one of those, right? If not, here I am!) I've made tons of mistakes and I'm not perfect. I'm still learning how to navigate my way through life – and every day, I'm getting richer for it (pun intended).

In just a few years, I've gone from being always broke and wearing clothes that are *literally* full of holes and held together with safety pins, to living a chilled, abundant life with my family. I earn awesome money, travel the world, can spend as much time as I like with my husband and kids, and I'm still a normal chick. Money hasn't changed who I am, deep down, but it *has* changed my life in every way.

Some days, I can't believe it's my life, and I know I've only reached about 10 percent of my potential. Earning money is fun now. It's just a game, instead of being an incredibly stressful and demoralizing experience. I've probably made every financial mistake possible. I want to reiterate that *I'm not perfect.* I'm just your everyday woman and mother, having an imperfect, perfectly human experience.

Here's my other disclaimer: I'm not a financial expert. I'm not an accountant or a debt counselor. I don't give (nor am I *qualified* to give) financial advice. You're not going to get spreadsheets here (well, okay, there is *one* in the bonus section on my website – see below); nor will you have to do complicated math (I still use my calculator for everything, even simple sums). I'm not that kind of coach or financial advisor. I can't tell you how to invest your money, or how you should pay off your debt.

However, I can honestly tell you that I've got a Goddess-given knack for helping women like you achieve your biggest and craziest dreams. I'm a money mindset coach, and I'm a really awesome one.

Getting over your money "stuff" will help you to not only earn more, but give you the confidence to pick the best – First-Class – team to help you invest your money. That means you won't spend it all, or sabotage your success.

I've helped women cut through years of under-earning and chronic underserving, to fly through their income goals. I've helped women heal *just one* memory from their past that unlocks everything else. Decades of old self-beliefs can shatter in a day, and release you to earn more money. The past can heal in an instant – and honestly, that's how you become rich. You're going to learn how to do all that in this little book.

✦ You'll realize it's not about the money at all.

✦ You'll see how money is just a symbol for *everything else* in your life.

✦ You'll discover which parts of your life need a drastic upgrade now or later, and you'll start to manifest the money to pay for it all. It's going to be fun, I promise.

So, my new best girlfriend, *are you ready?* The instant you start to second-guess yourself or put the book down, I want you to forgive the mistakes you've made up until now and get excited that your world is about to change. Like, seriously, get excited – because it's finally *your* time to manifest everything your heart desires.

It's time to be wealthy, loaded, well-off, prosperous, cashed-up, well-to-do, well-heeled, bling-blinged-up, and affluent. Whatever your version of being wealthy is, together we'll design it for you.

You are smart enough. You are ambitious enough. *You* are enough, and you deserve to be as wealthy as you want, *now*. Let's go on this amazing journey together. Let's get rich, lucky bitch! It's your time and you're ready for the next step! Love, luck, and abundance,

Xx Denise

Denise Duffield-Thomas
Money Mindset Mentor and Queen Lucky Bee
www.DeniseDT.com

To join the Lucky Bee network and get full access to the bonus section (all the extra resources I mention in this book, and other goodies we couldn't fit in here), make sure you register for free at www.DeniseDT.com/Rich. Do it now!

Chapter 1

Becoming an Amazing Money Manifestor

> *"The only secret of wealth creation is knowing how to use Cosmic Ordering."*
>
> STEPHEN RICHARDS

'm going to teach you how to become an amazing money manifestor. It means that you'll be able to create money at will, whenever you want or need it, *and* that you'll enjoy the process. It sounds like a big promise, but I can assure you that when you follow the steps, it works. No exceptions.

Some women seem effortlessly lucky, but they are just more experienced in following the laws of the Universe. There's no magic pill, and nobody is really born luckier than anyone else. It's just like how the fittest women are usually the ones who go to the gym regularly and are more consistent with their diet (lucky bitches!)

Manifesting is simply the art of transmuting a thought (a dream or a desire) into reality so that you can touch and experience it for real. It's not just about having a great mindset. Yes, you can work on having a "millionaire mindset," but it doesn't always translate into actual dollars in your bank account (maybe you've noticed this!)

When I read and watched the worldwide phenomenon *The Secret*, I thought it was amazing; but I was totally confused about what to actually *do*, being a practically minded Virgo. Like, do I just meditate on what I want? Do I have to wish *really, really, really* hard? Will I win the lottery if I think about it all day long?

I was obviously doing it wrong, because I was still broke. It was incredibly frustrating, to say the least. I felt like an idiot – being a self-professed "personal development junkie" but not being able to make it work in my bank account.

Like many ambitious, entrepreneurial women, I went on a journey of self-discovery to try and find the secret to money. I walked on hot coals while chanting "cool moss." I went to countless personal development seminars. I listened as dodgy internet marketing salesmen sold me their "System to Riches." And I tried to push through my blockages with sheer willpower and hard work. Sound familiar?

I loooooved talking about money in the abstract sense, and I devoured any book with "millionaire" in the title. But again, I want to reiterate: I was broke and tens of thousands of dollars in debt. More importantly, I was completely and repeatedly sabotaging my earning potential – so I was money *repellent*.

Now, this isn't one of those stories where I say I was homeless on the street, stealing TVs for crack money, and then I turned it all around to become a millionaire overnight. I was just your everyday chick earning a low-to-okay salary in a corporate job, with a couple of credit cards, personal loans, and a fairly hefty overdraft. I lived paycheck to paycheck. I could afford to feed and clothe myself and lived an okay life, but I *felt* poor.

Like you, I didn't want to be *ordinary*. I didn't want to live in my small, cramped apartment on the outskirts of town, full of cheap Ikea furniture put together (badly) by my non-handy hubby. I didn't want to walk to work in the rain, or worry about paying the bills. Most of all, I didn't want to depend on *anyone* for money, especially not a man.

I wanted to be *rich*. I wanted to walk into a fancy store, buy whatever I wanted, and wear awesome clothes. I wanted more than one pair of black shoes and one second-hand winter coat. I wanted to vacation in cool spots, and I wanted to prove to the world that I could make a huge impact and get rewarded for it monetarily.

So, while my friends were climbing the corporate ladder, I spent my time going to conferences and reading abundance books. I felt like there was a missing puzzle piece, though. There *must* have been something I was missing.

The *idea* of manifesting was awesome, but I needed to know the specifics and the logistics. What should I do next? *And then what?* Is there an order I should follow? Am I doing it "right"? *Where's my money?*

Now, as a coach and mentor to thousands of ambitious, entrepreneurial women around the world, I'm constantly asked questions like:

- Denise – what affirmations are the best?
- What's the right way to make a dream board?
- How should I word my goals?
- How many times a day should I write out my goals?
- Which works better: Emotional Freedom Technique or Access Consciousness?
- Do subliminal meditation CDs really work?

Here's the answer: Try it all. It *all works*. My philosophy is *throw everything at it*. It's your life, and your dreams deserve to be fulfilled – no matter what it takes. You'll hear personal development gurus say that *their* book, system, or process is the only right way, but that's total BS.

There's no perfect way to word your affirmations, and there's not *the* definitive dream board software. Everything that you do compounds over time and helps you to achieve your goals; you just have to be consistent and persistent in manifesting your wealth. Don't get too caught up in *one* particular tool being the silver bullet that will change everything. Not even this book.

Of course, just doing random stuff willy-nilly doesn't work either: there's definitely a flow you should follow. My manifesting process isn't the *only* way, but I know it *works* – not just from my own life, but from the awesome women I mentor on a daily basis. Those women create miracles and make progress far faster than the average woman – even the ambitious ones who grit their teeth and try *really* hard. Trust me: it doesn't have to be that hard.

All the personal development tools work, but it will take more than one thing, *done only once*, to activate the Law of Attraction. What you're doing is consciously manipulating time and space to help you achieve your dreams. You're literally rearranging the Universe in your favor. You don't need a magic wand or a Tardis to shift the Universe, but it's not going to happen by wishing on a star or lighting an abundance candle either.

Becoming a conscious manifestor requires you to *practice*; and honestly, most people don't have the discipline to practice enough to achieve mastery in anything. Just as with any worthwhile skill, it won't be effortless straight away. I can't be bothered to learn to play the piano because I don't have the patience to learn or practice. I'd love to be a good singer, but I have a *really* crappy voice, and it seems too hard to take lessons to learn to be good at it.

Manifesting is the same, and yet a lot of people get pissed off that it doesn't work the first time. Spoiler alert – you might not manifest a million bucks the first time you try. I know, right? If only! I seriously wish I could go to the gym once and have my dream body, but life doesn't work like that.

I know you understand this intellectually, but somehow most of us forget this truth when it comes to money. Instead, we start making up stories – such as "The Universe doesn't like me" or "I'm obviously not meant to be rich."

When I was manifesting my goal of traveling for six months, I tried *everything, every day*. I did it all – visualizing, goal setting, EFT tapping, journaling, forgiving, dream boards, etc – to make my dream into reality.

The Universe had an interesting way of bringing the opportunity to me – via a travel competition. But I wasn't trying to manifest a competition – I just wanted to go traveling, and I was willing to make it happen no matter what. It's like the competition got swept up in my desire – not the other way round.

Every day, I made at least ten to twenty little subtle shifts to tell the Universe that I was serious about wanting to travel the world for six months with my husband. Before I even knew about the travel competition, I got *obsessed* with my goal.

All up, I'd estimate that I tried more than fifty personal development tips and tools to manifest that goal. For the specifics, I encourage you to read *Lucky Bitch* as well as this book. It's an awesome story, but it also shows how consistent you need to be when you're consciously manifesting a life out of the ordinary.

That's why most people live a life of mediocrity: always settling for an Economy-Class life and never setting or reaching big income goals. Most people are just not willing to put in the work to live an extraordinary life, just like I'm not willing to put in the effort required to become an amazing singer.

Sure, I'd love to wave a magic wand to sing like Adele without having to actually *do* anything. When it comes down to it, though, it's obviously just not important enough to me to make it happen, no matter what.

I know you're different. You're reading this book and following the steps because you *do* have that burning desire, and you *are* willing to do what it takes. Don't worry. You don't need to follow a complicated system, or learn to meditate for five hours a day. I figured it out for you, so you can just relax and follow the process. It's worth it. It's really awesome being a wealthy woman, you'll see.

> *"The most popular labor-saving*
> *device is still money."*
> PHYLLIS GEORGE

Honestly, most people are pretty passive about their goals. They let life happen, vaguely hoping for a lottery win to get them out of their financial reality. I'm not criticizing. I've done it myself.

Some months, I set a really big financial goal and then do *everything* in my power to make it happen. I'm on top of my manifesting game and riding the wave. Other times, I just wish money would fall into my lap without any effort on my part at all. It's human and it's normal. But staying conscious about it means you acknowledge that you're doing it to yourself, and that you can snap yourself out of it.

In between manifesting big goals, I sometimes get lazy and let some of my daily manifesting activities slide. So, in response, the Universe is slow and apathetic about manifesting my goals. Some days it's so easy to manifest money: it's flying into my bank account so fast, I'm amazed.

Then I'll get complacent and think I can skip a day or two of my manifesting exercises. After a while, the fear sets in, and the money dries up. It happens every time. When you follow the process (or not), the results are fairly predictable.

Don't think that because I'm the "lucky bitch," I don't have to work at it. I do.

The gym analogy really is perfect here. When you're in the zone with your health goals, it feels easy – not only to work out, but to eat healthily too. You feel unstoppable! But when you've skipped a few days (or weeks) of the gym, or you've been eating like crap, it feels sooooo hard to go back.

So, it might sound like a lot of hard work and frenzied activity to *actively* manifest your ideal life and become rich. Once you've read this book, though, you'll see that there are just a few key shifts you need to make. After that, the rest are the little subtleties that will grow your income even further. Once that happens, it becomes a fun game. You become acclimatized to wealth, and then it becomes part of who you are.

There's no doubt that manifesting requires patience and constant vigilance to stay positive and in the right frame of mind. But once you have the hang of it, and start to see the results, you get quicker and stronger, and it becomes self-fulfilling.

It's just like your body has muscle memory: each time you get to a new phase of money consciousness (even if you backslide and go back to old habits), just follow the system again and you'll get back on track easily.

It's easy to get "dirty" energetically if you skip a few days of your good money habits, but that's normal too. You don't get immunity for life – a good money mindset requires daily consistency.

> *"People often say that motivation doesn't last. Well, neither does bathing – that's why we recommend it daily."*
>
> ZIG ZIGLAR

The Money Manifesting Formula

In a nutshell, here's my five-step formula for manifesting money (or anything else):

Step 1: Declutter everything in your life.

Step 2: Decide exactly what you want.

Step 3: Surround your life with positivity.

Step 4: Take inspired action.

Step 5: Receive and fine-tune.

This formula can be used to manifest literally *any* goal in your life. I obviously teach it in my Manifesting Course, but I also use it as the framework for my Money Bootcamp and even my ill-fated "Get Hitched, Lucky Bitch" Soul Mate course. (I ditched this one when I wanted to focus exclusively on money and business – big lesson in being focused!)

Literally, you could read this book again and substitute "love" or "weight" for "money," and *still* get incredible results. It doesn't matter if your goal is *huge* or tiny. You can use this formula to manifest your next car, a new job, five new clients by Thursday, your future husband – *anything*.

I've used this formula with clients to help them manifest things, including:

✦ A positive court case outcome.

✦ $5,000 within 48 hours.

✦ A husband and a baby for a client who was single for seven years.

- ✦ A dream dance job on a cruise ship.
- ✦ A new dream house in record time.
- ✦ A quick house sale to avoid foreclosure.
- ✦ Forgiveness with a family member.

As you practice using the formula, you'll start to receive what you ask for: even money. Simple as that. You don't have to be incredibly smart or particularly lucky to follow it – it just takes practice.

The best thing is that you won't just manifest "stuff" – the way I did when I started winning scholarships and prizes. When you follow the steps with a particular focus on money, it will become effortless. Money will start coming in from everywhere. I know this because I've witnessed it with my Money Bootcamp participants – it's unbelievable how the money starts rolling in.

Whenever I write a new book or course, I write down the five steps of the Manifesting Formula and design it with that flow in mind. When I'm stuck on my own goals, I just go back and mentally check off the steps, to make sure I'm not missing anything.

The formula is designed as a continuous cycle: if you get to Step 5 and your goal hasn't yet manifested, go back to Step 1 and start again. There's *always more* to declutter, and always more to clear. You can get *even more* specific; you can take *even more* inspired action; and you can practice the art of allowing *even more* abundance into your life. It seriously works every time, if you follow it.

Each step contains different practical and metaphysical exercises, which we'll cover in this book. Plus, if you want to go deeper into this topic, I have some life-changing resources for you, and a bonus section around the five steps that I couldn't fit into this book. So make sure you register for those at www.DeniseDT.com/Rich.

Remember, this isn't a university assignment. It's not some massive test you have to pass. You don't have to be a certain weight, color, age, or profession for this to work. It works for everyone. So keep asking yourself, *Why not me too?*

When it came to manifesting success, and especially money, I had my own self-limiting beliefs. I thought I'd have to become a completely different person – certainly a skinnier, nicer, more organized, and "perfect" person. But I'm here to tell you – *YOU ARE ALLOWED TO BE RICH*, no matter who you are. Sorry to shout, but I want you to get this. You don't have to wait until some mythical time in the future when Mercury Retrograde is over and the stars align perfectly. You can be ready *now*.

Got that, girlfriend?

My Manifesting Formula is not an intellectual exercise that you need to sit with and analyze to death. The thing with the Law of Attraction is that just *thinking* it isn't enough. You have to *feel* it, and every cell in your body has to *believe* it. You have to get into the space of living abundantly before the means to live abundantly actually show up in your world. You might have to fake it at first, but that's okay – because it still works!

> *"When riches begin to come, they come*
> *so quickly and in such great abundance,*
> *that one wonders where they have been*
> *hiding during all those lean years."*
> NAPOLEON HILL

I remember reading that quote and I was like, "But *when*?! I want it *now!*" I was sooo impatient to start living a First-Class life, but when I look at the Manifesting Formula now, I realize that I really wasn't following the steps. I was doing the equivalent of sitting on the couch, eating donuts, and getting frustrated that I wasn't skinny. *Universe – why don't you want me to be thin?!* (munch, munch). Exact same thing.

Winning that round-the-world trip was the turning point for my belief in my own manifesting power. Since then, I've continued to manifest amazing things from my dream board. Every time I break through an income goal, I go back to Step 1 and work through the steps again to break down the barriers to the next stage. Honestly. I don't get any shortcuts just because I write about this stuff. New goal = back to Step 1. Every time.

I don't have any magical power, either. I just work the steps, exactly the way you will. These strategies have worked for women all around the world. I've shared my manifesting secrets with more than one million blog readers in 169 countries; and more women are breaking through their own limits every day. It *will* work for you too.

My Manifesting Formula provides you with practical techniques to start bringing more actual money into your life (again: it's not just about teaching you how to win competitions and lucky door prizes). You'll learn to be open to receiving more money in your life – not just rely on being really lucky. Ironic, I know, but I believe you make your own luck.

It doesn't matter where you're starting from, or whether you grew up rich or poor. We're going to unravel all of your complicated money stuff and clean the slate, so you can create a new, healthy money relationship and get some actual cash in the bank.

By the end of this book, you'll have set some non-scary – but exciting – financial goals. You'll also know which way you're headed, and what you need to do to achieve the wealth you want.

We'll remove all of the hurdles on your path to being rich. Plus, we've got some "Denise Real Talk" on dealing with negative people, self-sabotaging behavior, and some of the inevitable snags on your road to financial awesomeness. I promise you uncensored truth bombs on what it *really* takes.

I'll show you how to take back your power around money in all situations, and teach you how to be chilled with your wealth and feel safe as a rich woman. I'll share inspiring stories of normal women just like you who got more open to receiving money, and are now on their way to becoming rich. You're in great company in the Lucky Bee community!

Really, manifesting is such a simple, predictable process, even though it deals with metaphysical concepts like:

✦ Manipulating time and space to your will.

✦ Becoming a reverse paranoid (believing that the whole world is conspiring to help you).

✦ Doing some, quite frankly, weird-ass sounding rituals.

It doesn't really matter whether you believe in the Law of Attraction or think it's a pile of new age poop. It still works. I've worked with some total skeptics who tried to convince me that they were different, and that their issues were so *unique*, it wouldn't work for them. It did work for them, and it will for you too.

Just follow the steps. Are you ready?

CHAPTER SUMMARY

❖ The Money Manifesting Formula recap:

~ Step 1: Declutter everything in your life.

~ Step 2: Decide exactly what you want.

~ Step 3: Surround your life with positivity.

~ Step 4: Take inspired action.

~ Step 5: Receive and fine-tune.

❖ Manifesting is the art of transmuting a thought into reality in the real world. Basically, it's about taking things off your dream board and turning them into something you can smell, touch, and experience. Just remember: manifesting = make real.

❖ If something isn't manifesting quickly enough, you've probably skipped a step. Trust me on this, and go back to Step 1.

❖ Throw everything at it – it's your dream life, after all!

Chapter 2

A Life-Changing Money Habit

*"There are people who have money,
and people who are rich."*

CoCo CHANEL

*B*efore we start putting the Manifesting Formula into action, here's some "pre-work" that will support your new relationship with money. Think of this as being like an underlying principle of everything we do in this book.

You might think that you're ready to take the reins of a multimillion-dollar fortune *now*, but in reality, you need to get intimate with what's already in your life. You may be thinking, *Um, I already know my money situation, Denise: I haven't got enough!*

Trust me, this might be the case for now. To get yourself ready for more money, you've got to be a good steward of every penny, cent, or dime that comes into your life *now*. This is a really important lesson, and it's one that has changed my life and the way I feel about money.

Acknowledge every cent

Let me tell you a harsh truth: you can't manifest money when you feel broke. You might think I'm missing the point – after all, why would you be reading this book if you already had all the money you needed? But that's the frustrating paradox of the Law of Attraction. You'll only get *more* of what you've already got.

Keep Track of Your Money

Here's the daily habit that will change your relationship with money. If you take nothing else away from this book, do this one thing:

Starting today, keep track of the money that comes into your life.

Track *every cent* – whether it's from your salary, gifts, money found in the street, bonuses, or an inheritance. Big or small, track it every single day; and most importantly, feel good about it. This will truly change how you feel about money, and attract more of it to you like a magnet.

> Your money tracker doesn't have to be fancy. I have several free resources in the book's bonus section on my website (including my personal money tracking spreadsheet) that will help make it easy (download yours from www.DeniseDT.com/Rich).

With this exercise, you're starting to train your awareness to look for more money opportunities. Every woman I mentor is way more abundant than she actually thinks she is, and I bet you $100 that you're exactly the same.

By paying close attention to all those extra little bits and pieces of money that come your way, you'll start to activate the Law of Attraction. Remember: like attracts like. So the more money you realize you have, the more money will start flowing to you.

On the other hand, if you only focus on how you lack money in your life, you literally send the Universe poor vibrational energy, and attract the same thing – a lack of money! That's why, when you're feeling really broke, you end up getting unexpected bills in the post or receive a speeding fine. You just attract more misfortune.

It's also good to track everything else of value that comes into your life that might not be actual money. These could be gifts, savings/discounts, or things that you receive for free. By taking note of these things, you might realize that you actually get more free stuff than money, and that you might need to switch your focus to manifest more money.

Remember how I said I used to win things all the time? I only realized the disparity when I started to track my money. When I saw that I'd manifested more than half a million dollars' worth of freebies in a year (but hardly any real *income* that I could spend), I knew it was time for a change.

No, I wasn't looking a gift horse in the mouth: free stuff is always great, but I wanted the experience of actually *paying* for things myself. I knew I wanted to go to the next level of wealth and responsibility.

Make a commitment to track your money every single day for at least a month, because *what gets measured gets improved*. It's just one of the laws of the Universe.

> *"The person who doesn't know where his next dollar is coming from usually doesn't know where his last dollar went."*
>
> UNKNOWN

Here's the truth. I started tracking my income when I wasn't making much of it. Over the next few years, I became incredibly good at making money. Now – with a multimillion-dollar business – I still track my income *every single day*. I actually check my bank accounts and update my money tracking spreadsheet multiple times a day.

As I said in the previous chapter, though, I don't get a "Lucky Bitch" pass from the Universe. If I stop recording and tracking my money every day, I manifest less of it. I start to freak out about my money goals for the month and receive less – because the Universe doesn't appreciate being ignored.

When I track my money every day, I make more. I'm excited about my abundance and appreciate every cent that comes in, so money is attracted to me. Simple. Plus, when you're aware of what's coming in, it's a wake-up call to take more action. You might get motivated to send out more invoices, to follow up with potential clients, or to chase unpaid debt. Remember: what gets measured gets improved.

When you do this exercise, you'll be surprised how much money comes into your life unexpectedly; and also how much you discount your current level of abundance. You don't have to have fancy accounting software or know your profit and loss. Good bookkeeping systems are definitely important, but this money tracking exercise doesn't replace them – it's a completely different thing.

You can use a simple piece of paper to track your money or download my free tracking resources (see above), depending on the format you like best. Don't think you can only start when you have a "perfect" system. That system doesn't exist, so it's just procrastination.

Dealing with your money doesn't have to be scary or confusing. Just know how much money you're already manifesting, so you can attract more. You gotta get intimate with your money.

> *"I'm so naïve about finances. Once*
> *when my mother mentioned an amount*
> *and I realized I didn't understand,*
> *she had to explain: 'That's like three*
> *Mercedes.' Then I understood."*
> BROOKE SHIELDS

Tracking your money is incredibly important if you've been frustrated about not hitting a financial goal. Chances are that you already hit it and didn't even realize, which makes you seem incredibly ungrateful to the Universe. Why give you more if you can't even acknowledge what you're getting?

Kerry Rowett, a kinesiologist on my Money Bootcamp, told me: "I realized I only feel that the money that comes through my account is 'real.' So I disregard money in my PayPal account, or money that comes as cash (even though it's recorded for tax purposes)."

This is so common. This feeling of money not being "real" is what derails most women from feeling truly rich. When we discount income or abundance "that doesn't really count," we're actually *pushing away* more money. Where in your life do you have rules around what's worthy of being counted or not?

Kat Loterzo, a personal trainer turned business coach, had no idea she was already hitting her big income goals when she started doing my Bootcamp. "I started doing my money tracking sheet, with a goal to manifest $20,000," she said. "I finally went and backdated every cent I'd received that month, and I'd already passed the halfway mark. I had no idea!"

Since then, Kat has created a million-dollar business, and she still tracks her income daily. *Tracking works.*

Kerry and Kat's stories are not uncommon. Women are notoriously bad at acknowledging themselves. As a gender, we honestly suck at claiming our power around money. The act of tracking money daily has increased Kat's income tenfold since she did the Bootcamp. She had the skills before: she just didn't realize how she was holding herself back from being paid beautifully for them.

Tracking simply gives you the information that you need to hit, exceed, and adjust your goals as you get better at manifesting and keeping money. If I had to ask you how much you earned last year, last quarter, last month... would you be able to tell me? *Honestly?*

*"I don't want to make money, I
just want to be wonderful."*

MARILYN MONROE

Many women tell me they want to be rich, but they are actually completely ignoring actual money. When I started working with my own money mentor, Kendall Summerhawk, I was too afraid to ask her a question about my business, in case she asked me how much money I made. I honestly had no idea!

It was awesome when, just six months later, I stood at a microphone at her annual money conference and proudly told her I'd earned $17,000 that month. For the first time in my life, I actually tracked my money without being scared about it. Knowledge is power; and honestly, tracking has played a huge part in allowing me to increase my income over the last few years. It will for you too: so starting today, track everything.

Frequently asked money tracking questions

I get more questions about this exercise than I do about any of the more complicated ones! I understand you want to get it right, but it's pretty simple. Any type of money tracking is going to be better than none, but that said, here are a few of the most common questions I hear.

Should I wait until I'm actually making money before I start tracking?

No! It's the whole chicken and egg thing. You're not going to be aware of your abundance until you track what you already have. You're probably not going to make space for more until you appreciate what you're already bringing in. And you might be surprised by the reality of your situation, compared to the story you're making up about it.

Do I track my partner's income?

Yes and no.

No if you're reading this book so you can learn to manifest for yourself. A lot of women are awesome manifestors… for other people. For example, you might set a money goal and then your partner gets a pay increase or an inheritance. That's just another form of hiding from money. If you're attracting money *through* your partner, then for the next few months, *only* track what comes to you alone. That way you can adjust accordingly, and focus on receiving abundance for *you*.

Yes you can track your partner's income too if you want to work with them to create even more abundance as a couple. You can always encourage your partner to track for themselves, too – especially if you like some healthy competition. See who is best at manifesting income goals each month. Have a competition to see who can find the most money in the street!

Should I track expenses as well?

I'm a big fan of knowing what you're spending, and having great bookkeeping systems, so if you already track your expenses, keep doing it. This, however, is not an accounting exercise: it's about awareness and appreciation. So for the purposes of tracking, start with what you bring *in* to increase your money manifesting ability.

That doesn't mean you should go crazy on your budget and spend more than you earn. It just means that, for this book and in my courses, focus on what you want to grow. It's unrealistic for you to try a million exercises all at once, so if you're picking one simple thing to do – track your incoming money first.

Remember: I'm not a debt counselor or a financial planner. My focus is on improving your mindset around money and helping you to feel rich. Please talk to your accountant about creating good money systems for tax purposes.

Do I really need to track everything?

Yes, track everything that comes into your life. Money is money is money. I get questions all day long in my Money Bootcamp: "Denise, do I track rental income?" or "But what about...?"

Yes, again, money is money. It all counts. Whether it was easy or hard. Whether it was something you worked for, or something someone gave you. Whether you felt like you'd "earned" it or not. Stop trying to discount your abundance by second-guessing it.

Every little bit counts, too. So when you find a penny in the street, pick it up, kiss it (physically or mentally!), say, "Thank you, Universe," and then track it! I'm totally not above picking up money in the street – I love it!

For how long should I track my money?

Track forever. Do it every day, whether you're earning very little or multi-millions. This amazingly simple habit can take you into riches. Even my multimillion-dollar mentors track their money every day – maybe they just switch to daily totals rather than tracking each sale individually, but they still know what they make, almost to the penny.

More questions on tracking? Spoiler alert – the answer is probably: "Yes, that counts!"

CHAPTER SUMMARY

❖ Track everything that comes into your life: every single cent and every bit of value. Tracking shows the Universe that you're paying attention to the abundance already in your life, and you'll start to attract more.

❖ All money counts. Pay attention to where you compartmentalize money as "real" or "doesn't count."

❖ To help you with this important daily habit, I've created some bonus tracking resources for you. I use these both in my personal life and for the students in my Money Bootcamp. Download your preferred method of tracking, and have fun updating it every day with every bit of money and value that comes into your life.

Get your free tracking resources from www.DeniseDT.com /Rich.

Chapter 3

Can Everyone Really Be Rich?

"Money without brains is always dangerous."

NAPOLEON HILL

*B*arbra Streisand once said, "Success is having ten honeydew melons and eating only the top half of each one." That made me laugh, *and* it triggered me a little. She truly is a rich, successful, and accomplished woman – but as you'll see from this chapter, there are *many* ways to be rich.

The Napoleon Hill quote above implies that only smart people *should* have money, but I've found that intelligence has got nothing to do with wealth creation. I know many highly intelligent, funny, talented, and generous women who are broke. I've also seen people grow rich on "dumb luck," and every combination in between the two.

So, how can you know what qualities are shared by *truly* rich women, especially if you don't know any women like that yourself?

At one of my live events, I got the participants to look at each other and say: "This is what a wealthy woman looks like." Because honestly, there is *no* obvious commonality. That means anyone (even you, especially you) can be rich. Go try it. Find a mirror and say to yourself, **This** *is what a wealthy woman looks like*. It might trigger you, or it might blow your mind to think *"Why **not** me?"*

When you put rich people on a pedestal, it's tempting to think that if only you had their exact traits, you could emulate their success. But guess what? Rich people aren't perfect. They're flawed, just like anyone. And they make the same mistakes as "normal" people.

To show this, we can look at celebrity women. Why? Because they're human just like the rest of us, but their money wins and woes are more public – meaning we can look at their stories and learn from them.

You might not personally know anyone who's won the lottery, and you might only know of a handful of truly wealthy people. Celebrities, however, are a handy example of what happens when people get rich quickly – and sometimes unexpectedly.

Although celebrities are usually above average in the looks department, they're probably no more intelligent than you or me. That's why we can learn a lot from them in how they handle their cash.

The problem is that most of the celebrity headlines seem to be about babies and breakups, and you rarely hear a celebrity talk candidly about money. Yes, you can look up the highest-paid actresses this year, which cast members just renegotiated a record salary, or who is going bankrupt, but how often do you hear celebrities actually talk about how they *spend* or *save* their money? And what happens when you're so rich you literally *can't* spend it all?

I would love to hear Oprah Winfrey talk about what it's like to open her bank statements, or to ask Meryl Streep about her investments. What about the starlets who find themselves multimillionaires in their twenties? How do they cope with the expectations of their family? Do they ever feel guilty about the money? I'm so curious about it!

When actress Jennifer Lawrence shared so openly that she had worried about being called a bitch if she negotiated for a higher salary for her work on the 2013 movie *American Hustle*, it was like a revelation for me. More money doesn't solve the underlying money blocks. Fear doesn't go away when you have money blocks. That's why some people never feel like they have enough.

Honest money confessions are rare. Maybe one day in the future, I'll have my own talk show where celebrity women can share their money blocks. If I ever do, I guarantee you that those blocks will be exactly like yours. It would be fascinating, right?

Lessons from rich and poor celebrities

Watch any tacky reality TV show, and you'll see famous celebrities from the 1980s and 90s who burnt through all their cash. It's almost fun to judge them for their excesses and poor decisions; but what if we have the same blocks, just on a different scale?

When I was first interested in money I'd read about Sarah Ferguson, Duchess of York, Courtney Love, La Toya Jackson, Judy Garland, Kerry Katona, Pamela Anderson, Mischa Barton, Amy Winehouse, Lindsay Lohan: the list of women who seemingly blew entire fortunes on shopping, bad divorces, alcohol, drugs, and lavish lifestyles goes on and on. Every generation will have its rags-to-riches stories, and we'll read about celebrity downfalls in the tabloids.

Looks like celebrities – with all their money, connections, and good looks – aren't any better with their finances than the average population. You might think, *If I had **her** money, life would be perfect*, but celebrities don't have it together either. Why not?

If you were to ask them, they'd probably say that their finances were mismanaged by their financial team, or stolen by their parents. That the economy was to blame. That they gave their wealth away to friends and family who took advantage of their generosity. Or they'd say that a million bucks doesn't go very far these days. Most of them would probably say they have *no idea* how it happened. Just like most of us do when we're in debt or have no money at the end of the month. Seriously, *where did it all go?*

How about we sum them all up with one blanket diagnosis – *money blocks*.

Celebrity women don't have much in common when you really look at it – some were born rich, some poor. They are different ethnicities, and have varying degrees of talent and IQ. You could say that being in the public eye doesn't help you stay rich; but take an average neighborhood, and you'll find plenty of similar stories – just on a different scale.

In my Money Bootcamp, everyone's background is *totally* different. You might think that if you'd only grown up rich, you wouldn't have money problems. *Wrong.* The exact same blocks hit women who grew up in completely different circumstances.

So there's nothing inherently "wrong" in your background that can stop you from being rich. There are just the stories you made up about it.

> *"I'm an athlete and I'm Black, and a lot of Black athletes go broke. I do not want to become a statistic, so maybe I overcompensate. But I'm paranoid. Oprah told me a long time ago, 'You sign every check. Never let anyone sign any checks.'"*
>
> SERENA WILLIAMS

Even though the figures are different, I'm guessing the issues that plague celebrities are the same ones that hold *you* back. The ones that keep you from hitting the six-figure mark in your business, from keeping more of your income, and from living the life you've always wanted. Piling more money on top doesn't deal with the underlying money issues.

That's why it's so awkward when women email me in desperation asking how to win the lottery – because I know that it wouldn't really help. It might sound like an awesome solution, but chances are, the money would be gone quickly for the same reasons that they're broke now. Money doesn't solve money blocks.

Some celebrities – not just women, either – seem to amass huge fortunes, while others get it and lose it just as quickly. There are lots of women that you'd assume were really rich, who are faking their lifestyles. Conversely, there are the "quiet" success stories.

For example, did you know that Judy Sheindlin has made more than $45 million from the syndicated courtroom show *Judge Judy*? The show hasn't changed much over the years (well, maybe she's got a slightly fancier robe), but at various points, Sheindlin was the highest-paid person on television, and the thirteenth richest woman in entertainment, according to *Forbes*.

She's earned more from her TV gig than Simon Cowell or David Letterman. Who knew?! I'm guessing that she's an amazing negotiator, because other women have been just as "popular" but earned far less from their talents.

Sofia Vergara, from the US TV show *Modern Family*, was quietly amassing a huge fortune too. In 2014, she was the highest-paid TV actor (not just actress). She earned more than Ashton Kutcher (the highest-paid male that year) and beat the #2 actress by $24 million.

That money wasn't just from her role on *Modern Family*. Girlfriend is a legit business *boss* lady, with her own fragrance on the Home Shopping Network and endorsements from Diet Pepsi, K-Mart, CoverGirl, Head & Shoulders, and more; plus she's the co-founder of Latin World Entertainment.

I'd love to hear about her money blocks, but I reckon she feels pretty good about herself. My lesson from Vergara is *leverage*. She took an ensemble role on a hit TV show and *ran* with it.

When I went researching for rich celebrities, I found only two types of information: the bragging and the downfall. The first type was announcements of large movie-star paychecks, often not validated by the celebrities themselves (and apparently a bit of a PR move). The second type was page after page of bankruptcies, and sad stories about celebs blowing it all. Obviously, the media love to see people humiliated and knocked from their pedestal, and this will never stop.

I guess it's boring to report on fiscal responsibility, and celebrities probably don't want to talk about their money fears...but it would be interesting, right?

It used to be really rare to hear a celeb brag about his or her lifestyle (except on that show *Cribs*, which was unusual at the time). Now, though, you can go on social media and see a newly minted celeb showing off his or her top-of-the-line Rolls Royce (in reality leased, borrowed, or sponsored), or Instagramming their crazy shoe closet full of thousand-dollar high heels. But you'll rarely hear them talk about their money lessons. They seem to be very shy on the topic.

I found plenty of cautionary tales though, and you have to read between the lines to find the beneficial money lessons that apply to you and me. Because honestly – and I'll say this over and over again – having more money doesn't change your underlying beliefs around money.

I'm incredibly grateful that we can learn from these celebrity women. The lessons are especially valuable if you don't personally know any rich women in your own life. I didn't know any wealthy women at all before I started to do this work.

I didn't know how to act with money, except what I saw on TV and in movies. Honestly, there aren't many good role models out there, so I see that we Lucky Bees have a responsibility to normalize wealth for other women in our lives.

Real-life celebrity money lessons

This headline is from the website ThisIsMoney.co.uk: "A £90k wedding, 15 pairs of designer Ugg boots, and luxury holidays: How Tina Malone's Shameless spending made her bankrupt."

Malone, the star of the UK TV show *Shameless*, explained how she's a sucker for sob stories, and how her "over the top generosity" in buying gifts for friends and taking her family on all-expenses paid holidays led her to bankruptcy.

She earned a healthy annual six figures from the show, which isn't an astronomical sum in the celebrity world. However, she spent it as if she were a millionaire. It's the exact same tale we hear when someone blows their lottery winnings.

Maybe you haven't taken your family on luxury holidays, but you might bail out your sister when she's behind on her rent – even though you're in debt yourself. *Why does anyone need 15 pairs of Ugg boots?* you might think, but maybe your spending addiction is something else (ahem, crystals...). The numbers might be different, but the blocks are the same.

It's easy to judge celebrities, but between the lines is a common tale that stops women from being wealthy: being over-generous. It's a tale of giving to others before we give to ourselves. Mothers, especially, tell me that their family has the best of everything, while they sacrifice and give to themselves last.

More on that in a moment.

Have you heard of the pop singer Limahl? The NeverEnding Story guy? Well, I hadn't until I saw him featured in a "celebrity money story." He was friends with

Elton John in the 1980s, and blew all his cash before his pop career fizzled out. The "feast and famine" cycle is incredibly common for celebrities and normal people alike. So is sabotage.

Often people think, *If I could just get a big windfall, my life would be perfect.* Nope. If your behavior stays the same, it doesn't matter how much money you make.

Some one-hit wonders rake in the cash for years, while others spend it just as quickly as their song was in the charts. The number one song the day I was born was My Sharona, by The Knack. That song still makes guitarist/songwriter Berton Averre an awesome amount of money in radio, television, and movie royalties every single year.

"It is far and away the major part of my income stream, and somehow it just keeps going strong," he told Australian news website ninemsn in an unusually candid interview about money.

To be fair, it's an awesome song, and I hear it on the radio all the time. Still, it's unusual to hear about how people make their money, especially when similar success stories have completely squandered their opportunities.

Remember the one-hit wonder song Gangnam Style? Korean pop sensation Psy had made more than $16 million from it at the time of writing this book. That figure has doubled since I wrote the first edition of *Get Rich, Lucky Bitch* – and it's probably growing every day! If he's careful, Psy can turn that one-hit wonder into a sizeable nest egg.

Or he could blow it on lavish spending, like 80s rapper MC Hammer, who burnt through his $30 million fortune on an expensive entourage and outrageous spending. I laughed when I saw Psy and MC Hammer perform together at the

2012 American Music Awards with a Gangnam Style/2 Legit 2 Quit mashup. Maybe MC gave Psy some financial advice in the green room? "Hey man – save some of that one-hit wonder cash, okay?"

I know this is bordering on depressing, but here are some more examples of celebrity money gone bad.

Anna Nicole Smith – a model for Guess in the 90s – got a massive inheritance from her billionaire husband, but she died broke when his kids sued for a reversal of his will. Cautionary tale – *don't marry old dudes for money.* It's not the best financial plan in the world, and you can waste a lot of years between wedding and funeral. So it's not worth the risk, in my opinion. There are easier ways to make money!

> *"Don't marry for money. You can borrow it cheaper."*
> Lois P. Frankel

I read about a lady called Patricia Kluge who at one point set the record for the largest divorce settlement ever. She went through a reported *billion dollars* on large, gaudy jewelry, paintings, and vineyards. Lesson – *keep some money for a rainy day.* Again, those numbers are bigger than they are for most of us, but that sabotaging behavior is the same.

My mother, at fifty-five, got a small cash windfall; and even though she needed major dental work, she bought a motorbike (yes, really, an actual motorbike), which she rode once, got scared, and sold for a loss a year later.

I'm not immune from it either: when I was twenty, I bought a $250 men's vintage tuxedo because I got a bonus at work, even though I was still eating cheap pasta for every meal. Basically, sometimes we make irrational decisions about money – whether we're rich, poor, or anything in between. More money doesn't automatically make you more responsible.

Some people feel really uncomfortable having excess money around, so they compulsively spend it. Many of my new Bootcampers feel bad if they end the month with even $5 of unspent cash – because they're used to being at zero. Part of the money lesson is learning to be okay with a buffer. To see whether this is a block for you, put your hand on your heart and say,

> ## "IT'S SAFE FOR ME TO HAVE EXCESS MONEY. IT'S SAFE TO HAVE A BIG SAVINGS CUSHION."

Actress Kim Basinger filed for bankruptcy in 1983 after a $20 million commercial real estate deal went south, and Main Line Pictures sued her for backing out of the B movie *Boxing Helena*. Again you might think, *If I had lots of money, I'd be so responsible with it!* Well, are you responsible now with the money you have? If not, change your behavior, and maybe you'll attract more money – plus you won't sabotage it in the future.

What about 1990s singer Toni Braxton? She should be as famous (and rich) as Mariah Carey and Celine Dion – she's certainly as talented – but she's filed for bankruptcy *twice* due to excessive spending, divorce, and illness.

When you think how much money Mariah makes from her Christmas covers *alone*, it's sad to hear that Toni ended up so broke. She had to sell her personal possessions, including awards she'd received, when she should be making more music and living off her royalties.

American Nadya "Octomom" Suleman (who first made headlines after giving birth to octuplets in 2009) made a ton of money doing her reality show in the mid-2000s. But just a few years later, she had to do soft-core porn to pay her bills. By the way, she did an amazing interview with both Oprah and Suze Orman in which they confronted her about her money situation. It's hard to watch, but it is enlightening and we can learn from it.

As I said, every decade is going to have cautionary money tales because people don't change. Have a look at who is making the headlines today. Same old money crap.

Again, the numbers are bigger for these celebrities, but the underlying principle is the same. I've seen many entrepreneurs have an incredible launch and make a ton of money, only to spend it all quickly or not put money aside for taxes. The money block can come from one of two key places:

1.   This hot streak will last forever, so why bother slowing down?
2.   I feel guilty about all this success, so I'm going to get rid of it as quickly as I can.

I know lots of really successful entrepreneurs who've filed for bankruptcy for mostly the same reasons, i.e.:

❖   Not taking responsibility for their finances.
❖   Putting their heads in the sand instead of dealing with problems.

◆ Being over-generous with others.

◆ Not saving any money for the future.

Some of these entrepreneurs are transparent about their problems, while others hide it from their followers. I'm not being a bitch here. It's easy to judge from the outside, but we can learn from it.

> *"We don't pay taxes. Only the little people pay taxes."*
> LEONA HELMSLEY, THE "QUEEN OF MEAN"

Who wants to be like that?!

If your only role models for being rich are from movies, then it's no wonder that you think you have to work really hard, or be a raging bitch to get there. Remember the *Friends* episode where Phoebe was a stockbroker who had two heart attacks while yelling into her phone? She was nice when she was a broke singer/waitress, but with just a bit of money, she turned into a total bitch.

There are a *lot* of examples of the rich bitch theme in TV and movies. Admittedly, I'm going a bit overboard here, but it's interesting to see what money messages go into our subconscious – and then play out in our lives – about what kind of women get rich. Humor me a little longer.

Think of the movies you remember from your youth. Goldie Hawn in 1987's *Overboard* was the rich bitch who threw things and yelled "I almost had to wait!" at her staff. She only became nice when she lived a life of poverty with hunky Kurt Russell and his ragamuffin kids.

Lesson – *money makes you spoiled and bitchy; poverty makes you humble and nice.* Well, if you've internalized that, you're going to have a huge money block around earning more money. It's better to be humble, right?

We had a saying in our family: "It's nice to be important, but it's important to be nice." It's like you can't have both – you have to choose one or the other. I had no idea how much that was ingrained in me until I went decluttering my money beliefs.

What about the noughties *Desperate Housewives* crew? Gabby was grasping and conniving, while Bree was domineering and had serious OCD. The "nice" ones, on the other hand, had the most financial problems and the messiest houses. Besides, the clue is in the name – they are mostly housewives married to rich guys.

Lesson – *you've got to marry to get rich.* I've heard that from ordinary women too: "If only I could find a rich guy to marry." Girlfriend, make your own cash!

> *"My mother always said don't marry for money, divorce for money."*
> WENDY LIEBMAN

If you watch any of the *Real Housewives of...* shows, you'll know they're exactly the same. It doesn't matter if the women are self-made businesswomen, they're mostly just shown as shallow, bitchy, catty, and incredibly ostentatious.

Again though, that's TV. In real life, it would be a boring show if they followed *me* around. I don't dress up in designer clothes or have impeccable makeup. But if you've never met a real millionaire, you might assume that you have to be like that to be rich. And if being like that goes against your very grain, well, that could be a possible money block holding you back.

One of my memories growing up was watching "rich girl" Cher in *Clueless*. She was sweet, but dumb and spoiled, and most of her rich friends were assholes. I had no other examples of "normal wealth."

Regina George in *Mean Girls* was a conniving bitch who stomped over everyone else in school. Alexis in *Dallas*, the rich brats in *Gossip Girl*, Miranda Priestly in *The Devil Wears Prada*, Cruella de Vil from *101 Dalmatians*, the women in *Revenge*... the list goes on.

The lesson for all of us?

Rich = Bitch

Rich women in the music industry are consistently reported as total divas. They're thought to make ridiculous demands (think J-Lo and Mariah Carey), to be aggressive perfectionists like Madonna, or madcap eccentrics like Lady Gaga. Look at who is being reported on today and the language being used.

J-Lo apparently required an all-white décor in her dressing rooms – with lilies and Jo Malone candles – plus both refrigerated and room temp water. Of course, the papers used words like "diva demands" and "outrageous requests." I actually really love room temp water myself, so I get you, J-Lo.

On the set of *Basic Instinct 2*, Sharon Stone apparently requested Pilates equipment, a chauffeured car driven by a non-smoking driver, two assistants, first-class travel, and a deluxe motor home with air conditioning.

What runs through your mind when you read that list? Do you think it's outrageous, or do you think she knew her worth? (Seriously though, how gross is it when you have to travel in a smoky car?!) She probably dealt with a lot of crappy conditions when she was starting out.

This is probably completely fabricated bullshit, but when Britney Spears performed in London's O2 arena in the early 2000s, she apparently requested platters of McDonald's cheeseburgers (with no buns), one hundred figs and prunes, and a framed photo of Princess Diana. Diva-licious!

Hell, I've even heard that the Queen of England required a brand new toilet seat at every location while she toured around the world. (So, apparently, does Mary J. Blige.)

Regardless of whether any of this is true, what's the message to the average woman?

Rich = Diva

These women are called "demanding" – despite the fact that they've gotten to the point in their careers where they just want life to be easy. What if, instead of being "demanding," they simply have great boundaries in place to ensure consistent standards, and just ask for what they want?

My experience in traveling around the world speaking and living in hotels is that it's *annoying* to try and do your job when you're surrounded by constant upheaval and change. If you hate feather pillows, are allergic to a certain type of flower, or get sick with unfamiliar food, shouldn't you be able to ask for what you need to do your job, without being called a diva?

I need a good latex pillow when I travel, and actually, room temp water is my preference. Wouldn't it be awesome if that was just taken care of for me? At my last live event,

I specified exactly what I wanted for lunch, and had an assistant whose job it was to refill my water.

I needed to give my best, and I couldn't do it without specifying what I needed. Did I feel like a bitch? Yes, at first – but I got over it because I knew the feeling came from an underlying block around "deserving-ness," and the belief that I have to do everything myself.

You're *not* being a diva if you ask for what you want.

Many businesses have a strict operating manual. Imagine if you were a McDonald's franchisee and you decided to go rogue and change up the recipes. Nope. Not happening!

So, if you're a performer and you're traveling around the world, why not have a strict operating manual, so each show is just as high quality as the last? Of course, the men who do these things are seen as "rock 'n' roll," but the women are just divas.

You'd assume that venues would take care of their guests, but without a manual in place, they probably can't because there aren't any clear instructions. Trust me: I bet these women have learned from experience to ask for what they want, and to *never* leave it to chance.

In her MTV documentary, rapper Nicki Minaj addressed the "diva demands" accusations so well: "I put quality in what I do. I spend time, energy, effort, and every fiber of my being, to give people quality. So if I turn up to a photo shoot and you got a $50 clothes budget and some sliced pickles on a motherfuckin' board, you know what? No. I am gonna leave."

Seriously – have you ever settled for metaphorical pickles? I know I have! I've been to speaking gigs where there was barely any tap water for the speakers, or a private place to get changed.

Nicki says, "Next time, they know better. But had I accepted the pickle juice, I would be drinking pickle juice right now."

Have you ever experienced the block in your own business where you felt like a bitch for correcting something, or asking for what you wanted? I used to feel bad even asking my assistant to do work for me! Many of us have never seen examples of healthy boundaries without them being depicted in a negative way.

The papers are also full of stories about successful, wealthy women in the corporate world; unfortunately, they are shown to be aggressive, greedy, too "busy" to have children, too masculine, or hyper-competitive. Female politicians are routinely described as "shrill" and bitchy, or even as witches. They are often judged on their looks and clothing, rather than the message of their politics.

The movies you watched in your formative years showed you that the only women in charge and successful are the hard-nosed, ice queen, money-obsessed, mean-to-the-underlings, bitchy bosses like Miranda Priestly in *The Devil Wears Prada*, Sandra Bullock's character in *The Proposal*, Demi Moore in *Disclosure*, Sigourney Weaver in *Working Girl*, and Jennifer Aniston in *Horrible Bosses*. And let me just say this here: it was actually hard to find many more examples, because so few women are depicted as leaders.

"Nice" bosses are usually broke-but-well-meaning women who run a sweet, run-down bookshop, florist, or shabby chic bakery – like Meg Ryan in *You've Got Mail* or Kristen Wiig's character in *Bridesmaids*. The message is that it's okay to be an entrepreneur, as long as you aren't making money out of it. When Anne Hathaway's character became good at her job in *The Devil Wears Prada,* she lost her boyfriend and her friend. The lesson that we're absorbing?

Rich = Ball-Breaker

Watch the messages in today's movies and shows (they are so much better, but still have a long way to go). Basically, rich women are shown to be:

+ Demanding divas
+ Spoiled
+ Mean
+ Bitchy to their friends
+ Overly competitive or aggressive
+ Pretty on the outside but mean on the inside
+ Conniving
+ Materialistic
+ Unethical
+ Horrible to people they perceive as "underlings"
+ Lonely
+ Much divorced
+ Shallow
+ Superficial

Apparently, rich women will henpeck their husbands, kill puppies, lie, cheat, poison, and steal to get what they want. They are gold diggers, tax evaders, wicked stepmothers, and evil queens.

Can you think of any *nice* rich women in the movies? Usually this happens only when they go out in the world and experience poverty, overcome a huge hardship, or are "rescued" and marry into wealth with a bland Prince Charming. Lots of these women are only happy when they finally ditch their pursuit of success and realize that "money isn't everything," or "love is more important than a career."

Holy crap. No wonder the message is so pervasive. I hear normal women say things like "I'd rather be happy than rich" or "Helping people is more important than money," all the time. Yes, of course – but in real life, you don't have to choose between the two!

Movies aside, if any of this is ringing true for you, take some time to deconstruct your fears about becoming rich – to find out where they're coming from. Even if you don't *think* you have any fears, play along; because trust me, there is *something* holding you back.

Giving away your power to others

In her book *Nice Girls Don't Get Rich*, Lois P. Frankel cites giving away power, especially to men and other authority figures, as one of the main reasons that women don't get rich. Unfortunately, we're often taught at a young age to believe that the men in our lives know more about money than we do.

Because of this, many women feel scared and intimidated to talk about it. Lois says, "Don't relinquish your say in financial matters in order to avoid bruised egos. If you do, you only lengthen the time it takes you to become financially free."

By the way, her book is excellent, and I highly recommend adding it to your financial success library.

That's probably why this is another example from the celebrity cautionary tales file – giving up responsibility to others. This one has ruined many a celeb, and can be a huge warning to a lot of women. Maybe you do it too? I certainly have.

Nowadays you hear about a lot of celebrity dirty laundry, but sometimes it was very hidden. Remember 90s girl group TLC? Their album *CrazySexyCool* sold more than 10 million copies, but the girls had to declare bankruptcy soon after because their contract meant they earned very little once everyone else was paid. They just assumed that their advisors knew what they were doing.

Have you ever signed a contract that you didn't really read, or agreed to something that you later regretted? I have. I've lost huge amounts of money on events because I didn't read the contract properly, or allowed my event planner to sign on my behalf. I've agreed to taking low percentages in joint ventures because I didn't want to negotiate better terms and look like a "greedy bitch."

Pop star Rihanna filed a lawsuit against her former accountants in 2014; apparently the firm took 22 percent of her tour revenues while she earned less than 6 percent. They represented her from age sixteen until her early twenties, when she finally fired them. Hopefully, she learned from that painful experience, but lots of us don't and repeat the lessons in different ways. Yes, we're talking millions with her, but remember, the blocks are the same.

That sounds crazy, until you realize that maybe you've done a similar thing. Have you ever paid everyone else in your business before you paid yourself? Agreed to a profit share that didn't take into consideration how much extra you worked?

I have, and so have many of my business friends and Bootcampers. But when you recognize it as sabotage, you can learn from it.

American Idol 2014 winner Fantasia almost lost her home to foreclosure, even after the life-changing opportunity of winning the #1 singing competition in the world (at the time). In her autobiography, she admitted that she was functionally illiterate, and was unable to read her contracts. She trusted her management to act in her best interests. Guess what? Nobody will act in your best interests better than yourself.

And ladies – we *have* to get comfortable with reading the fine print. Yoko Ono sued EMI for $10 million, claiming she was cheated out of royalties from John Lennon's estate. Who was giving her legal advice? Why didn't someone flag that for her?

In 2012, Lauryn Hill (the lead singer of the Fugees) pled guilty to tax evasion and faced a three-year jail sentence. Who was advising her on her taxes? Did she forget to put tax money away (as so many of us do)? Again, read the papers to see how common this story is today. Money blocks are timeless.

Yet again, the numbers might be bigger for these celebrities, but have you ever felt "cheated" out of your just rewards, or got your taxes in a tangle? In my first year of business, I filed my tax return late because I was so disorganized and didn't get information to my accountant in time. That wasn't just because it was my first year in business, either: experienced businesswomen are prone to procrastination too!

Many women just sign their tax return without really looking at it. Guess who gets in trouble when problems crop up during an audit? Not your accountant. You do.

A reality show star accuses her ex-husband of stealing all the money in their joint bank account and leaving her broke, despite all her TV show money. *How does that happen?* Well – do *you* know how much money goes in and out of your joint account? Do you have your own savings for a rainy day?

Many women believe that their husbands know more about money than they do. Or that they aren't good with numbers. This isn't true. This is a block to clear.

It doesn't matter how powerful or rich the celebrity, they aren't immune to giving away their power either. I found several quotes that made me think. For example, while searching the Telegraph.co.uk's regular celebrity money feature, I found these interesting nuggets:

From self-proclaimed "rich chav" Katie Price, aka Jordan – a former *Sun* newspaper Page 3 topless model and now an empire builder:

"Are you a saver or a spender?"

"I spend, but I have people around me who save for me. My brother and another guy look after my money. I don't know what I've got. At least I don't know to the penny what I've got."

Did that make you a bit twitchy?

And Australia's own Olivia Newton John of *Grease* fame:

"Do you use a financial advisor?"

"Well, I have a wonderful husband, John, who's a businessman. I feel more comfortable turning to him. He has my best interests at heart and I trust him. He's very knowledgeable, and I've learned a lot from him about running my business interests and my finances."

Argh, no, Sandy! But guess who has done the same thing? *Me.*

My husband Mark and I signed up to see a financial advisor just after our daughter was born. Honestly (and I say this without bragging... too much), we had to do this because my business had become so successful, we needed the extra advice. I'd finally become comfortable with having excess cash in my life – unlike the first two years of business, when I'd spent it all!

I was nursing Willow at the time, so when we went into the meeting, I thought, *If she cries, I'll go outside and leave the men to talk about money.*

Whaat?

It was essentially *my* money that we were talking about. (Okay yes, "our" money because we were married and had joint accounts, but I'd earned this "spare money" through my business.) Yet there I was, ready to abdicate decisions about it to the men because I assumed they could make better decisions.

Wake. Up. Call.

Within a few seconds, I went through the mental process that you're going to learn in this book, then took a deep breath and said, "Mark, Willow needs to be changed. Could you go change her while I tell these guys more about my business?"

In a way, it was a bit of a power move, but I needed to take control of my story asap – so I didn't sabotage my perception of myself as a powerful woman.

So, even though the examples of the celebrity women I've highlighted seem dated, human behavior doesn't move on. You could pick up the paper today (well, go online, but you know what I mean) and see the same stories. In fact, they are normal women's stories too.

Nothing is ever mentioned or admitted about bad financial management, poor decision-making, excessive shopping, or drugs and alcohol. The women simply trusted others to make their decisions for them or put their heads in the sand. Seriously, even though the sums are different, how many of us have done the same? Do you have money regrets from the past? All of us do.

Being a smart, successful woman doesn't mean you don't have money blocks. Have you ever thought, *If only I had more money, I could breathe easier?* Well, honestly, more money won't help if you don't deal with the underlying money blocks. Otherwise, more money, same problem.

Britney Spear's divorce papers from K-Fed showed that she spent practically all of her $737,000 income each month (yes, that's *monthly* income). It went mostly on rental properties for her and her family, entertainment, and restaurants. Yes, she'll still get royalties from her songs for years to come, but what happens when those royalties dry up?

How many of us live paycheck to paycheck? We think that if we earned more money, that problem would be solved, but it wouldn't. Even though we don't earn as much as Britney, the default behavior is the same, right?

Some women even think that they have to live close to the edge or they'll lose something essential to their work. They think that the adrenaline is a good thing that makes them hustle harder, or that their creative muse only shows up at the last minute. No. It doesn't have to be that way. That's an old story and you can release it.

Please realize that this celebrity feature isn't intended to make fun of anyone. Instead, we're using these stories as cautionary (and extreme) examples of what normal women do too. Basically, celebrities are just like us. They simply have higher incomes and greater extremes. They spend beyond their means, rarely save money, give away their power to the men in their lives, and make bad money decisions – just like we do!

I've heard the same thing many times from "real-life" women:

+ It's too confusing for me.
+ It's easier if he manages it.
+ I don't know where my money goes.
+ I don't know the first thing about money.
+ I'm always broke at the end of the month.
+ I hate dealing with the bills.
+ I have no idea how much debt we have.
+ Money stresses me out too much.
+ I don't open my credit card statements.
+ I just need more money – that would solve everything.

It can be tough to admit that you sabotage your money by giving away your power to the men in your life, or that you overspend on shopping, or that you're overly generous. However, self-awareness is the key to breaking free of old habits and allowing yourself to receive more.

The good news is that these realizations are also incredibly freeing and transformational. When you get rid of everything between your ears that's not conducive to earning money, and then follow the rest of the Manifesting Formula, it becomes (gasp!) *easy*. Self-awareness will set you free and give you lifelong tools to deal with inevitable challenges in future situations.

No joke.

I've seen this happen myself with all the clients I work with, and in my own life. For *years*, I tried to work for myself. I was a born entrepreneur, but I never earned any money for it. Yes, a dollar here and there, but nothing serious. Definitely not enough to quit my job, which I desperately wanted to do.

The month I decided to work on absolutely decluttering my life of every negative money belief and fear, I made $225 in my business.

Not impressed? Okay, granted, it's not that exciting. However, what you need to know is that it's more than I made in *18 months* of one of my "practice businesses" on the side of my full-time job. I celebrated every *penny* of that $225 because I knew it was just the start. It finally felt easy and fun, and I wasn't afraid anymore. (At least, I wasn't until I hit my next money barrier, but that's further along in this book. Don't worry: I'll share *all* of my embarrassing money stories, I promise.)

I had more decluttering to go, so I made it a game. The more I cleared, the more money I made. In fact, I doubled my income in the second month ($450), and then doubled it again ($885). I kept clearing my money beliefs (it becomes addictive when you see the results), and uncovering even more areas where I held myself back.

Each time I broke through an income barrier, I uncovered even more negative self-beliefs and fears. One big fear was that it was a fluke. The first time I made over $10,000 in a month, I honestly felt sick; and a little voice inside me said, *No further, this is as far as you'll go.*

I ignored it, and kept decluttering and following the Manifesting Formula. Soon after, I had my first $10,000 week, then my first $10,000 day, and now I've made multiple six figures in an hour. But I'll reach new limits and think the same thing: *This is it. No more for you. Who do you think you are?*

Just because I wrote this book, don't think that I'm perfect with money. I still work on my money blocks every day. More money doesn't give me lifetime immunity. There's always more work to do.

As David Neagle says, "New level, new devil." Each time you declutter an old belief, you'll break through something you previously thought was impossible. If you're stuck, you just need to do more decluttering work around what you believe is possible.

As I work through my money blocks, I keep making more money. I'm not ashamed to tell you that I make a *lot* of money now, and have even bigger goals. (If all these numbers are stressing you out, that's okay. Keep reading, and you'll discover exactly why.)

Guess what – I didn't get some fancy degree. I didn't suddenly become smarter. I didn't become a drug dealer. I didn't win the lottery. I just decluttered my beliefs around money.

Who are you trying to impress?

What about keeping up with the Joneses (or the Elton Johns, in the case of pop star Limahl)? Who do you try to impress with your money? Are there people in your life you feel inferior to? Do you ever go on lavish shopping sprees you can't afford in order to feel good about yourself? This one can be so tempting because we have access to so much cheap credit.

When I first moved from our tiny apartment to an oceanfront penthouse, I still kept my relatively crappy car. And even now, I drive a pretty moderately priced one that isn't exactly a typical "millionaire's car." Yes, I could buy something flashy, but I'm also realistic about my lifestyle – which includes carting around small kids and beach gear. I'd only be making this upgrade to impress other people, and that is the *worst* reason to spend money.

I can tell you from experience how expensive it can be to impress people. It took us three years to pay off our wedding – which we couldn't really afford at the time –because we wanted to impress our friends and family. We overcommitted to a huge venue, and then upped the guest list to fill it.

It's a common sabotage and probably the easiest to fall into – especially if you're friends with other people who spend beyond their means too.

When money makes you feel guilty

Let's talk guilt and money. I've heard from two separate friends how a sizeable inheritance made them feel so guilty that they blew it within weeks. One friend got a huge insurance payout after her brother died of cancer, and the money made her feel *sick* – as if she was profiting from his death. She blew it on a few holidays that she didn't even enjoy, instead of a down payment toward her first house (a big dream).

The sad story of 9/11 widow Kathy Trant is a classic case of guilt sabotage. She received $5 million in insurance payouts for the death of her husband, Dan, who had worked on the 104th floor of the World Trade Center.

According to the *New York Post*, she spent $2 million on home repairs and more than $500,000 to take friends and relatives on holidays. She also gave friends sums of $20,000 and $15,000 to pay off debt and buy real estate, and bought two women boob jobs (one was a beauty therapist she had just met).

It's a heartbreaking story because the money was frittered away on largely meaningless things, leaving her broke – and, of course, still grief-stricken. Can you imagine being in the same situation – how hard it would be to keep that money, knowing where it came from and why?

When people leave you money in their will, I'm sure they intend it to be enjoyed and used to provide comfort and stability. You can't manifest someone's death by setting big financial goals, and you're not disrespecting them or celebrating their death by spending the money in ways that will enrich your life. It doesn't disrespect their memory: it honors it.

Even just the *fear* that this will happen can sabotage your goals. I've had Bootcampers say they're scared to set big money goals because they're worried they'll cause a death and receive the money through an inheritance. Release this fear – and if you're really worried about it, add a qualifying statement, like *for everyone's highest good*, to the end of your goals.

But the underlying block is that *for money to come, something bad has to happen to balance it out*. That's not true, and you can declutter this one with the tools that come in later chapters.

I've personally seen people get large windfalls of money, only to blow it all on over-the-top presents for their kids or expensive crap (motorbikes, cars, jet skis, boats, etc.) that they can't afford to maintain; or by giving it away to others. It didn't bring them any long-lasting joy or security.

When this happens, it's self-sabotage, pure and simple. As tempting as the fantasy is, winning the lottery or getting a huge injection of cash won't solve anything.

We had one big example in our town. A local tradesman-turned-billionaire bought a private jet, a helicopter, sports cars, and lots of real estate within a very short space of time. Over the next few years, it was all repossessed – piece by piece – as he got sued, or filed for bankruptcy. Making lots of money certainly didn't make him a nicer or smarter person.

Going back to Jennifer Lawrence, she said there was a major reason she hadn't negotiated for more money on the movie *American Hustle*: "I didn't want to keep fighting over millions of dollars that, frankly, due to two franchises, I don't need."

You might wonder: *Why would you feel guilty about money?* But this is a really common money block, and it's usually completely unconscious. I've had Bootcampers tell me that they sabotaged going full out on their financial goals because they felt they should be happy with what they've already achieved. Others told me that they felt incredibly guilty about making "easy money" doing something they loved when other people were struggling.

I completely sabotaged a re-launch of my Bootcamp because I felt the same way. I didn't "need the money."

I wasn't going to starve if I didn't re-launch, so I kept procrastinating the re-launch.

You might think, *What a lucky bitch problem to have!* But trust me, this is a common block that happens at all levels of income. It's okay to have more than you need.

Should you give money away?

When I ask women what they'd do with a big financial windfall, the overwhelming response is that they'd give it away to friends and family. That sounds awesome, but let's examine some of the blocks that hide behind this seemingly generous gesture.

Being overly generous is a trait that plagues many women. What should feel good becomes an overwhelming need to be liked. What starts off as charitable turns into being bled dry. I believe in the power of giving, but when it comes at your own personal cost, it becomes self-sabotage.

I'm not even talking about charitable giving here. Are you always the first (or only) person to reach for the restaurant check? Do you lend money and never ask for it to be paid back? Do you feel overly responsible for other people's money dramas?

You might not be supporting an entourage of friends and family members, like some celebrities, but being too generous is often a disguise for your inability to receive from others. Giving shouldn't bankrupt you. Giving shouldn't block more abundance coming to you, or keep others from learning their own financial lessons. Don't leave yourself a victim by over-giving. Instead, make sure your giving feels good and still honors *you* and your financial goals first.

When it comes to lending money to friends and family, follow personal financial guru Suze Orman's advice. Don't loan money if you've got credit card debt yourself, prepare a written contract for repayment, and don't lend to enable someone else's poor money management. More money won't solve *their* money blocks either. You could give them all you have, but the sabotaging behavior won't go away.

> *"Men and women both have an equal capacity to make money, but they want money for different reasons. Men want money for power; and women want it for comfort, and usually not their own comfort, but the comfort of others in their lives."*
>
> SUZE ORMAN

By the way, I saw Suze Orman speak at a Hay House conference. She started her speech with "I stand before you a very, very, very wealthy woman." I loved that opening line because it was so inspiring to see a woman completely owning her power and not minimizing her success.

I've stood on stage and said the same thing, and encouraged the audience to say it out loud too. Try it, and see what comes up for you.

Suze understands that a lot of women feel scared about money, and I highly recommend her books. She says, "Don't panic. When the topic turns to money, so many women fall into a horrible default mode of 'I can't do this' or 'I don't know what to do.' I want you to commit to one month of telling yourself, 'Yes, I can.' That crucial change in attitude is the first step."

Many women sabotage themselves by thinking that they aren't smart enough to understand money. You are. You are smart enough.

Do you think that Sofia Vergara has been judged as "not smart enough" because of her boobs or her accent? You bet she has.

You might have your own BS excuses too. Maybe you failed math at school. Maybe you think you don't deserve success because you grew up a certain way. Nobody is born knowing how to deal with money – but you can learn.

As I said, earlier, I still use a calculator every day, because honestly, I suck at doing even simple sums. You have to declutter those pesky beliefs that tell you that you can't be rich because of X, Y, or Z (usually ridiculously silly reasons). *You* are what a wealthy woman looks like. *Why* not *you*?

Are you getting how important this is?

It's tempting to subscribe to the lottery win fantasy or the complimentary upgrade fantasy, but there are quicker and more certain ways to manifest money than winning it. You have *far* more chance of becoming a millionaire through your own ingenuity than through an arbitrary lottery win.

We all like to think that one day, we'll be at the back of the plane (having bought the cheapest ticket) and the stewardess will come up and say, "Grab your bags, you're going to First Class!"

I know this *does* happen occasionally, but it's rare for the person on the plane who has invested the least to be upgraded. Generally, airlines reward people who have a *history of investing in themselves*. That's why frequent flyers are the first to be upgraded.

Another way to look at it is this: God helps those who help themselves. You know this is true in life, and it's also been proved in studies. Read Richard Wiseman's *The Luck Factor* to see his studies of people who believe themselves to be lucky or unlucky. It's fascinating reading, as Wiseman confirms that luck is largely self-fulfilling.

> *"Happiness doesn't just flow from success; it actually causes it."*
>
> RICHARD WISEMAN

I remember one of the experiments in *The Luck Factor* vividly. The researchers placed a $5 bill outside the research center to see who noticed it and picked it up. Sure enough, the majority of the people who found it were the self-proclaimed lucky people.

Why? Some people are convinced that lucky things happen to them all the time, so they constantly anticipate good news and opportunities. Others are convinced that the world is against them, so they are always waiting for the bad news. Which group would you rather be in?

According to Wiseman, these are way you can become more lucky:

1. Maximize your chance opportunities

Build your network, have a relaxed attitude to life, and be open to new experiences. (This is exactly how I manifested the free travel experience. I had a big network of people and just "happened" to hear about the competition from a friend who knew about my travel goal.)

2. Listen to your lucky hunches

Take steps to develop your intuition, and pay attention to your gut feelings. (For me, this is time away from my computer, having some quiet space in my brain, and putting myself in situations where I feel rich. That's when my intuition feels enhanced.)

3. Expect good fortune

Expect good things to happen to you, keep going in the face of failure, and tell yourself that you're a lucky person. (When I'm in this frame of mind, it's amazing how many "lucky" things happen!)

4. Turn your bad luck into good

See the positive side of bad luck, and don't dwell on bad situations. (For me, this means becoming a "reverse paranoid," and assuming that *everything* that happens is ultimately for my highest good – even if it looks bad on the outside.)

Oh crap, you're thinking, *I'm not lucky at all!*

First of all, if you *think* you're not lucky, the Universe will go out of its way to *prove* it to you. If you're always saying things like:

✦ I'm so unlucky.

✦ Typical, another bill!

✦ This *always* happens to me.

✦ Why does the Universe hate me?

◆ Nothing good ever happens to me.

◆ Why can't I be lucky too?

I hate to tell you this, but you are creating it. Luck can be learned (isn't that why you're reading this book?), but it can take practice if you're used to being negative.

I'm not super positive all the time, but I'm pretty lucky. It's because I'm constantly saying things like this to myself, and others:

◆ I'm so lucky!

◆ Thanks, Universe, for taking care of me.

◆ Wow, another coin in the street – woo-hoo!

◆ An unexpected bill? This must be a message from the Universe to pay attention. Thanks!

◆ Good things happen to me every day.

◆ I'm so blessed and grateful.

◆ This always happens to me!

◆ You'll never guess what I manifested today!

See the difference? Lucky people are overwhelmingly grateful and take responsibility for their lives. The unlucky people, by contrast, are pessimistic and "hard done by." Even when something "bad" happens, I always look for the good – because my underlying story is that "the Universe is always looking after my highest good."

Actor Neil Patrick Harris agrees with me, saying: "A lot of people would take getting rear-ended in their car as an example of why their life continues to be one roadblock after another, and I think a different person can see that same fender bender and be grateful it wasn't worse.

"That allows them an opportunity to learn something from it – sort of take some sort of positive elements from that. I think if you try to angle your life in those ways, then fate, destiny, karma opens itself up to you and allows for more growth."

I've had car accidents in which that's exactly what I did. I thanked the Universe for the "wake-up call" to pay more attention, or to get a safer car.

Manifesting outrageous abundance requires vigilance toward your everyday thoughts about your ability to create luck and abundance. It means you have to be really careful about what you say to yourself and others about money.

At the beginning, it might feel forced – like you're just pretending to be happy – but that's okay! Pretending is like rehearsing for success, and your brain can't tell the difference anyway.

> *"If you ask how they make decisions, 'lucky' people will talk about tuning in to information and instincts, while 'unlucky' people often mention pushing away the uncomfortable feeling they were headed for trouble."*
>
> MARTHA BECK, LIFE COACH

I remember when I first read the book *How to Win Friends and Influence People* by Dale Carnegie – I think I was about sixteen years old. The most important points I remember were about:

1. Eye contact
2. Giving compliments
3. Mirroring people

So I started practicing. Even though it felt fake at first – while I was consciously maintaining eye contact and trying to think of something to compliment – after a while, it became natural and just something I do.

Ditto with the positive thoughts. It's only when you become aware of your negative thoughts and feelings about money that you'll be able to switch them around. It might feel like hard work at first – because it's a deeply ingrained habit – but then it will become second nature.

The two examples I gave above about lucky and unlucky people were pretty obvious ones, so don't assume that you've decluttered everything about money and skip to the next chapter. Your negative beliefs about your ability to be wealthier might be subtle but just as destructive.

That's where it starts to get fun, though! Imagine easily breaking through your next income barrier just by re-examining your thoughts about money. You don't have to get smarter, and you don't have to change gender, get a boob job, or grow three inches taller. You don't have to get skinnier before you deserve more money. You don't have to turn into an evil genius or do anything unethical.

> *"You and I are such similar creatures, Vivian. We both screw people for money."*
> EDWARD LEWIS (PLAYED BY RICHARD GERE) IN *PRETTY WOMAN*

The "rules" we have about ourselves and *when* we can actually be rich are kind of ridiculous. That's why, as you go through this book, I'll get you to ruthlessly examine your current beliefs about what you're capable of. I'll also teach you amazing tools that you can use to keep taking yourself through each income barrier as you work through the Money Manifesting Formula.

Seriously, knowing and mastering this stuff will make you feel like you've got a superpower.

What if becoming rich was actually easy?

For women, one of the very common fear about becoming rich is that you'll have your nose to the grindstone 24/7. That it will be such hard work that you probably shouldn't bother. That your kids will suffer if you get richer. Maybe you're already rapidly approaching burnout and thinking, *Another five, ten years of this to get rich? I'll never make it.*

Maybe you have an underlying story that there's a strong correlation between money and hard work. So, if you want to double your income, you think you have to work twice as hard. Wrong. In fact, that belief actually stops you from leveraging your business, outsourcing, delegating, or otherwise making it easier.

I've had clients who just couldn't seem to slow down. They felt like they should be working all the time because they believe it's the only way to get rich. So paradoxically, they never *felt* rich. They just kept running, running, running, and never getting anywhere.

> *"The easiest way for your children to learn about money is for you not to have any."*
>
> KATHARINE WHITEHORN

One of my Bootcampers, Jen, had a fear that being successful meant total sacrifice. Her dad had a low-paying job that he loved, but which caused tension in her family. He had opportunities to get paid more, but refused them because it would mean time away and longer hours. So, Jen did extremely well in her career, but burnt herself out trying to prove she was living up to her potential, unlike her dad.

To her, success was all or nothing, black or white. She believed you could either love what you do and not reach the pinnacle of success materially, or you could have a lot of money and a corporate job that was really stressful and a sacrifice to your family.

If I'm successful, I have to be ruthless and determined, you might think. Nope, you don't. You don't have to become Regina, Alexis, Cruella, Miranda, or any other kind of rich bitch. You can still be *you,* and be an awesome kind of rich woman. You just have to rewrite the script to suit your dreams for your life.

You can choose to be rich *and:*

- ✦ Philanthropic
- ✦ Gracious and friendly
- ✦ A great role model for women
- ✦ A leader and mentor
- ✦ Inspiring to others
- ✦ Generous to people around you
- ✦ A creator of amazing experiences
- ✦ A world explorer
- ✦ An angel investor

You can create scholarships with your money. You can build the most eco-friendly, technologically advanced house in the world. You can buy big chunks of the world's rain forest. You can explore the world. You can be an amazing role model for your kids, your family, and your community. *You can change the world.*

You can choose to be like author J.K. Rowling, who gave away so much of her money that she dropped down from the *Forbes* billionaire list to a mere multi-millionaire.

What about Oprah Winfrey, who has created amazing things with her wealth? She created her Angel Network, which inspired philanthropic giving all around the world, and her school for young girls in South Africa. Nobody can dispute Oprah's legacy as one of the world's richest women.

Hey, and it doesn't have to be all about *giving away* all your money, either. It's okay to keep it and use it for fun and pleasure. It's totally okay to live the most outrageously luxurious life you want. We're told that it's "good" to give and "bad" to spend money on ourselves, but it's up to you how you'd like to spend your money.

You could fly around the world on your private jet to see Adele in concert. (You could probably hire Adele to sing on your private jet, just for you.) You could have a private butler take care of your every whim in Zanzibar. (I've experienced this, and it's awesome.) You could buy a $100,000 dress to wear to the Oscars and then auction it off. You could take off on a round-the-world cruise with other rich people, or buy an island, or meet up with your fellow Lucky Bees to see Bette Midler in Vegas.

You might be thinking, *Oh, but Denise, that's so ostentatious, so greedy, and just **way** too decadent!*

The point is, gorgeous, *nobody* can dictate to you what kind of rich person you're going to be. There are many shades of wealth. There are billionaires who dress like hobos, millionaires who drive twenty-year-old cars, middle-class people who go on spectacular holidays, average people who have cleaners and private chefs, paupers who live like kings on credit cards, and everything in between.

There's no rule that you have to be a rich bitch. Only you decide what kind of wealthy woman you become.

> *"I'd like to live like a poor man*
> *with lots of money."*
> PABLO PICASSO

I'm okay with being a real-life inspiration for other women, but you don't have to be like me, either. I'm just one example of a rich woman: it's up to you to design *your* First-Class life. By the end of this book, you'll have a much clearer picture of what you want.

For awesome rich girl inspiration, check out Beyoncé's social media. You'll see photos from her daily life in all its luxurious glory. Girlfriend is enjoying her wealth, and she was plenty rich enough before marrying Jay Z.

Or browse luxury travel or real-estate sites. Even ones that make you cringe. Sometimes I'll follow someone crazy and ostentatious to see what emotions it brings up for me, so I can clear the triggers. I don't aspire to be a rich asshole, but it's not a good emotion to hate them or begrudge them their wealth either.

Role model other amazing wealthy women, like Ellen DeGeneres, Sara Blakely (the creator of Spanx), Martha Stewart, Sheryl Sandberg, Diane Von Furstenberg, Anna

Wintour, Tyra Banks, or Gisele Bündchen. Read their autobiographies, or – if you get the chance – see them speak. Find amazing philanthropists to model by reading *Forbes'* annual rich lists.

Your financial role model might be your grandma or your local female politician. She doesn't have to be a billionaire or a businesswoman: instead, she could be someone you really admire for her values and grace in the public eye, like Michelle Obama. Basically, follow in rich women's footsteps, and you'll feel good about being rich too.

Turn your attention to great stories of wealthy women (and men); and ignore the negative ones about the guilt of working mothers, lengthy court battles over wealth, nasty divorces, and rich women acting just as greedy as the greediest man. Most of that stuff is a distraction that can make you feel fearful about wealth. Engaging in debates designed to fuel the "mommy wars" is just as destructive. Ignore it all.

Join us in the Money Bootcamp and you'll see real women, just like you, upgrading their life every day. Just like you, every one of them has her own tastes and values around what's important to her. Or you may not know what you want yet. It can take practice to actually decide what you like, rather than what you think a "rich woman" would spend money on.

Inspire yourself by reading books about successful women, and you'll see how they overcame their own struggles with negative people, how they built up their self-confidence, and how they made and spent their money.

How can you learn the lessons from these celebs, and not make the same mistakes? Don't worry or get depressed that you'll sabotage your wealth too (and therefore not even try to become wealthy). There are a lot of positive examples of awesome rich women with healthy relationships with money, and we'll cover them in this book.

However, we'll also look at why we sabotage in this way, and how we can give up our sabotaging behavior to create a beneficial, abundant relationship with money – no matter how rich we get.

You know that annoying quote that every personal development guru spouts: "The definition of insanity is doing the same thing over and over again and expecting a different result"? (Or as my husband Mark puts it: "The definition of insanity is hearing the same quote over and over again.") Well, in this case, it's true. It's ridiculous for anyone to expect their financial circumstances to change without changing the behavior that got them into that circumstance in the first place. So that's what we're going to work on together.

You don't need to become famous to be wealthy, and I'm not going to ask you to rob a bank or do anything unethical either. That said, this first step – uncovering and then decluttering what's holding you back – can be tough for some people. In fact, I spend about 80 percent of my work with my Money Bootcamp participants in this step, and it can be uncomfortable.

That's why I'm glad you bought this book. It's a great introduction to living a richer life and dealing with these very normal money blocks.

However, it's just the start. Learning to become rich is a lifelong process; and it's one that will require you to ruthlessly declutter all the things in your life that don't serve you (mainly beliefs and self-sabotaging behaviors). You'll also need to constantly examine *why* you're acting the way you do. It's about giving up the victim mentality and accepting that only *you* are responsible or to "blame." Are you willing to do what it takes?

It's your time and you're ready for the next step.

CHAPTER SUMMARY

❖ Celebrities and rich people have money blocks, just like you do.

❖ You can release the stereotypes of what rich women are in the world, and create your *own* meaning of wealth.

❖ Choose your money role models carefully, and ignore the bad ones. You can be any type of rich woman you like.

❖ Sabotaging behaviors are normal, but you do need to be honest about yours.

Get my Top 10 list of must-read money books for women in the bonus section at www.DeniseDT.com/Rich.

Chapter 4

Declutter your Money Stories

"Taking responsibility for your beliefs and judgments gives you the power to change them."

BYRON KATIE

When I mentor my Money Bootcamp participants, we spend more than 80 percent of our time on decluttering old beliefs and cleaning up sabotaging money habits – so we can figure out *why* we act the way we do. This part is just the uncomfortable crap you have to wade through before things can be easy.

We've all got our own money dramas, and maybe some of the celebrity money stories from the last chapter hit a little too close to home. Have you identified your major money sabotages yet?

Are you:

+ Over-generous?

+ Overspending to impress other people?

+ Mindlessly spending to make yourself feel good?

+ Spending out of guilt or obligation?

+ Saving other people from their financial dramas or problems?

+ Giving away your power to other people in your life?

If you've identified a few areas where you're sabotaging yourself, fantastic! The more self-aware you can be about your money behaviors, the better and the quicker you'll move to the next income level.

Think of it as a game of Snakes and Ladders – when you engage in self-sabotaging behavior, you slide down the snake and go backward. When you acknowledge and clear those beliefs, you get to climb the ladder and make fast progress.

Like most things in your life, the way you handle money has a lot to do with your past experiences and what you've seen or learned while growing up. This is true whether you grew up rich or poor. In fact, there's no correlation between your family wealth and how many money blocks you have!

Everyone, at any income level, can be abundant or feel poor. Our perception is way stronger than the actual reality. But do you believe that you – with all your blocks, sabotages, and experiences – can be rich? Do you believe that you're just as deserving as anyone else?

Imagine that you have your own personal river of abundance that can never run dry. It can flow to you all day and night with *everything* you need to live an amazing life. However, only a trickle of that abundance can ever get to you if the river is blocked. Think of your negative beliefs around money as massive boulders, and imagine each negative money memory you have blocking up the flow even more.

If you're downstream of the river, you can only see a tiny trickle coming to you. So you think that's all the abundance there is, not realizing what's in the way. But that trickle represents such a small amount of what's available to you, and the only way to access it is to remove those self-imposed barriers by identifying and destroying them forever.

Luckily, the tools you'll learn in this book will help you to dissolve even the biggest obstacles. Trust me: I've seen it all and heard every story. Nothing is so bad that it can't be released.

You might believe that your income stems only from your actual situation right now – how smart you are, how hard you work, etc. But honestly, it's most likely that your *past* experiences with money influence your income more than anything that you're doing today. These stories formed your money beliefs, and your beliefs influence how you make decisions in your life and business today. They also underpin most of your sabotages.

You might have had a childhood where money was really tight, so you've got funny-but-kind-of-sad stories about your cheap-ass dad, or the Christmas when you got the most awful present ever. Perhaps that's why you now overspend for your own friends and family – in an effort to exorcize those yucky, embarrassing memories.

Or maybe you had rich parents who spent money like crazy. Maybe you had a rich uncle who paid for everything, or a friend who was really poor and made you feel guilty for having money. Either way, you unconsciously push money away now as an adult, by making bad financial decisions in an effort not to be the "rich bitch."

Your past experiences have shaped who you are today, and they might be holding you back from becoming your best and wealthiest self. When you do radical emotional decluttering on those past money experiences, though, you can start with a fresh new perspective on money, and allow your natural abundance to flow.

Emotional decluttering is a non-negotiable process if you want to be rich. Even if you've done it before, try it again with a specific money focus, because there's *always* more to uncover. In the world of manifesting, negative emotion is really the only thing that holds you back.

You can try to skip this step, but it's like building a beautiful mansion on top of a trash heap. That gorgeous home will topple over at the slightest hint of bad weather; and it'll probably have an underlying stench the whole time, so you'll never enjoy it, even while it's standing. You have to excavate and build a strong foundation first if you want your mansion to last.

Look to Your Past for Clues

If you want to earn more money, you must release *any* negative energy you have around it – no matter how small.

You have to be willing to look at any memories from your past that have an attachment to money – especially events where you felt angry, sad, embarrassed, or humiliated.

Find *any* memories of old arguments or resentments over money, or anything that might possibly explain why you act the way you do now with your money.

Go through your life chronologically. Start from your earliest memory about money, and work your way up. Trust me: this exercise will change your life, because you'll see how clearly these memories influence your income today.

The first time I did this exercise, I wrote five pages' worth of stuff that I still felt angry about. There were bosses from years back who didn't give me a pay increase (those bastards!); anger toward a family member for a cheap, crappy birthday present; and my stepdad and his strict rules around pocket money.

Some of that stuff was *years old*, but on some level, I was still thinking about it. You can bet that decluttering it all gave me permission to rapidly increase my income. The only reason I could even make that first $225 was that I started decluttering my money memories. But I didn't want to get stuck at that income level, so I kept going and kept forgiving. And I still do it. You'll uncover new memories all the time as you grow your income.

And you know what? When I tried to replicate that original list a couple of months later, to see if there was anything left, most of it was gone. I had let it go: I was over it, and I was free of it. *Forever.*

Holding on to the energy of money drama is incredibly subtle but dangerously destructive. You might not think you even *have* any money drama left from your life. Well, you'd be surprised. Most women have at least a few major incidents around money that affect them as adults today.

What do you remember about money?

You could have all kinds of money memories that affect the way you think about money as an adult. For example, you might have felt angry when someone stole money from you in the sixth grade. Maybe it embarrassed and humiliated you; and that feeling of shame and helplessness still lives within you today. So you don't entrust people with your ideas, and never ask for help in case someone steals your success.

Or you could have stolen money from someone else, and that memory makes you squirm because you're still carrying the shame and guilt of the "thief" tag. You might not think about it every day, but trust me: it's still there. It makes you feel guilty for no reason, and makes you feel overly responsible for mistakes that simply aren't your fault.

Maybe you felt poor when you had to wear an old suit to a job interview. You remember vividly how it felt to hold yourself in a certain way so a stain or rip wouldn't show. It made you feel inferior to all the well-dressed people around you. That version of yourself still lives inside you sometimes, and that leftover whiff of inferiority holds you back from being rich because you still have an "Us vs Them" perception of rich people.

Maybe you were embarrassed for a friend because she was short of cash at university, and it was excruciating every time the restaurant check came. Your compassion and empathy for her actually caused you to feel her emotions for her, and *that* is still living inside you.

Embarrassment is such a powerful emotion when it comes to money. You could be embarrassed that you're rich, or embarrassed that you're poor. And it doesn't always have to be about being broke – you could be embarrassed that your parents were wealthy and you didn't really "earn" your success.

> *"Money, if it does not bring you
> happiness, will at least help you
> be miserable in comfort."*
> HELEN GURLEY BROWN

Think about your career. Were you ever unfairly denied a pay rise? Does it still hurt when you think of the *injustice* of it? Maybe you found out that you were paid less than a coworker, and it seriously pissed you off, but you couldn't say anything. I would lie awake at night rehashing old conversations with my old boss and get *so* angry years later.

The rehashing isn't good for your blood pressure, and it's not good for manifesting money either! It's unnecessary mental clutter, and you could use that energy to create something amazing in your business or life.

What about your relationships? Remember any money situations that relate to your boyfriend, girlfriend, partner, or ex-partners. You should get some juicy memories around them; and trust me: those memories are *still* living with you and affecting your income today.

One memory that came up for me was about a boyfriend I had at university. He was a real tightwad. He would order all this expensive food in restaurants and then he'd be really cheap when it came to the check. We went out to dinner with my mother, and he told her, "You had the prawns so you should pay more!" And this was the first time they met.

Who wants their daughter to be married to someone like that? I had another boyfriend who always spent all his money on cigarettes, but expected me to buy him lunch and even help him with rent, even though I was a student and was super broke. And I did it too!

So both of these memories went on my money clearing list, because you can bet they both brought up feelings around being worth spending money on. The things you remember might be small, and you might not see the connection at first glance – but don't take any chances. If you still remember something with *any* kind of emotion, it's something you should clear. Remember – throw *everything* at it.

If you want to get good at manifesting, you have to stretch yourself to see the connections. It's the equivalent of practicing your scales to master the piano. Clearing these little memories adds up to mastery of yourself, and responsibility for your thoughts.

You can go on adding to your money forgiveness list as much as you want. Anyone and anything related to money that still gives you an emotional charge should go on it. It doesn't matter how small or large the memory, you're doing a deep clean and leaving nothing to chance.

Creating the list could take you anything from ten minutes to hours and hours. As you go through this book and you remember new things, I encourage you to keep adding them to your money forgiveness list. It's not something you do once and then just forget about. I still add situations and memories to my list. My income is different, so I see some of the memories through new eyes, but they still give me hugely valuable insights.

Forgive... and Set Yourself Free

Okay, so you have your list, even if it's just a few memories long at first. The hard part is almost over – because most people put off actually writing their list in the first place. I applaud your bravery and commitment to your own personal development.

There's no need to burn the list or do any weird Voodoo rituals. Just clear it through energetic forgiveness. I bang on about forgiveness all day long, for one simple reason – it works miracles in all areas of our lives, and it allows the money to flow naturally.

Here's what you do: go through each item on your list, one at a time. Take time to think about that incident and what it meant to you. Let any residual emotion come up.

Then simply say the forgiveness mantra: "I forgive you. Thank you. I'm sorry. And I love you." (This is based on Ho'oponopono, the gentle Hawaiian practice of reconciliation and forgiveness.)

You can say the four elements of the mantra above in any order that feels good to you. I had someone tell me that I was "doing it wrong" because she was taught another order. Seriously, though, you can't screw this up, as long as your intention is to release and declutter the memory. It's so simple.

Note: Don't think that because this exercise is simple, it's not going to work. It's incredibly powerful stuff, and it will change your life for the better!

Emma Pointon, a photographer from Adelaide, shared this in my Bootcamp. "I started my forgiveness exercise this morning. It made me feel physically sick while doing it; but after, I felt lighter. I think that the process will have to be rinse and repeat, rinse and repeat. There's lots to clear, forgive, and release to the Universe."

It's normal to feel sick, resistant, and even headachy after this exercise. Some people definitely have that reaction. But it's worth continuing so that you can clear the memories and make way for more money. Those memories are better out than in.

You might say: "I'm not going to forgive that asshole. Are you serious?!" Okay – it's your choice. All I can do is share with you the complete transformation that thousands of Lucky Bees have experienced purely through the power of forgiveness. Money mantra: "The more I forgive, the more money I earn, because I allow myself to receive."

Make forgiveness a regular part of your life. Parisa Eithne Roohipour, a yoga teacher in Vancouver, told me,

"Sometimes I do forgiveness in the shower, so I feel like the ickiness is being washed down the plughole."

Just like brushing your teeth and washing your hair, forgiveness can make you feel squeaky clean every day, and *worthy* every day. When you feel worthy, you can attract money easily.

So keep going over the items on your forgiveness list until they have no emotional charge anymore. Some things will be gone. You'll forget them forever. They'll just be lifted out of your heart and soul to make room for other, lighter emotions. Some memories will stay with you and take longer to shift.

I told you I was going to be straight with you. Here's the honest truth – you'll probably have to do the forgiveness process again and again, and probably for the rest of your life. It doesn't mean you spend your whole life doing it. It just means that every time you hit a new money block, you go back to forgiveness – the process is that powerful.

Be more persistent than your ego, which wants to believe that you're right in being pissed off. Your ego wants to hold the grudge, but do you want to be right or *rich*?

Are you ready to let go and forgive?

Forgiveness is one of those things that people always try and skip, because it just seems like either too much hard work or totally unnecessary. *Denise, I'm reading this book for wealth strategies, not this airy-fairy crap!*

Forgiveness is like childbirth – you can't bargain your way out of it if you want to get through labor. My mother told me that she totally forgot the pain of childbirth... until she was having my brother. At that point, she remembered how painful it was, and kept trying to bargain with the midwives:

"No, no, I don't want to have a baby today, I think I've changed my mind." And the midwives just said, "Sorry, it's happening whether you like it or not."

Forgiveness is usually scarier *before* you do it, but the end result is so worthwhile. Without it, you can't move forward. Still, it's completely normal to think, *No, it's going to hurt! It's going to be messy and ugly. I don't want to do it – don't make me, Denise!*

So while it might be painful to do this exercise, and there might be some tears, it really is worth doing. (Seriously, I can't emphasize this enough!) Plus, in addition to strengthening your manifesting muscle, forgiveness and emotional clearing will leave you lighter and happier, and open the flow of your river of abundance even more.

Give up the guilt

At various stages throughout your energetic journey to more money, you might come across one of the most common feelings women suffer – guilt. You might feel guilty for wanting more, for spending money on yourself, or for taking time out of your busy family life to work on improving yourself.

You might feel guilty that other people are poor, that your friend is jealous, or that there are starving people in the world. Many women on my Money Bootcamp start to feel guilty that it's suddenly really easy to make money. I *definitely* had "the guilts" when I increased my prices to well beyond what my colleagues were charging, and more than my friends or family earned.

We women are guilt-ridden creatures. And the answer to this, again, lies in forgiveness work.

No one can make you feel guilty without your consent

One of the questions I'm most commonly asked is "How do I stop feeling guilty when I'm in debt?" I often hear comments like "I don't deserve to spend money!" But people who say that don't do things that are *free* to make themselves feel good either – like using their best china or perfume. So their guilt doesn't go away with more money.

In my experience, guilt is mostly a female thing. Many successful male entrepreneurs (of all types – at extremes that run from ruthless capitalists to generous philanthropists) have gone to the brink financially many times. They've gambled on their business success with credit card debt and huge bank loans, and then let their various businesses go bankrupt if they weren't successful.

These guys have pasts littered with the carcasses of forgotten or failed business ventures. "That's business," you'll hear these types of men say. "It's not personal." I don't think it affects their self-esteem in any way – or their capacity to grow more wealth.

Well, for us women, it *is* personal; and I bet you've got some failures from your past that you're ashamed of too. Most women would rather die of shame than go bankrupt and not pay their suppliers. Most women see past business failure less as a valuable business experience, and more as a personal failure. They think, *I'm obviously not good at business.* I see lots of women quit over a perfectly normal rite of passage, like their first hater or a less-than-spectacular first launch.

> *"What we perceive as a failure may
> simply be our inner being's way
> of telling us that we are ready to
> move to a new level of growth."*
>
> ANNE WILSON SCHAEF

Forgive yourself for past business failures. You tried your best, and it was only a practice for the next thing. It's a journey.

So, in the spirit of "come at it from all angles," I listed every single business failure I've had: from the embarrassing (having a dismal multilevel marketing business) to the ill-conceived (my Raw Brides business in my late twenties, where I helped women lose weight for their wedding with raw food – despite hating weddings and not being a health expert), and even my little business ventures as a kid.

I figured that if any of those failures still followed me around in any way, it wouldn't hurt to release them in order to make way for new and profitable business ideas. So I forgave them all.

Take it one step further. Forgive your old business partners; and forgive the companies, suppliers, customers, and agencies you worked with. While you're at it – forgive the taxation department, the bankers, the government, the economy, and the president or prime minister. You might think that's going overboard, but it can't hurt, right?

> *"Letting go gives us freedom, and freedom
> is the only condition for happiness."*
>
> THICH NHAT HANH

The beautiful thing with doing this multilayered work around forgiveness is that it eliminates any feelings of guilt and unworthiness in your future businesses that could repel customers and opportunities. When you forgive yourself and others, it gives you permission to do more, have more, and be more in your life, without sabotaging it all through guilt or unworthiness.

Think of all the celebrity examples in the previous chapter. Imagine if they'd released all their old money stories and allowed themselves to enjoy their success.

Even if you've failed in the past, you can give yourself permission to earn money easily now. I remember really early on in my relationship with Mark, I had this big guilt trip about buying new clothes. I would only shop at second-hand stores; and while there's nothing inherently wrong with that, it didn't make me *feel* in alignment with wealth.

I didn't believe that I deserved to have the exact size, color, shape, and perfect fit that you can only find in brand new clothes. I believed deep down that I only deserved to have cast-offs; and that I had to settle for what other people had thrown away.

I remember walking the street with Mark past a shop window, and he would say, "Oh, don't even look!" because we were so broke. He would put his hand over my eyes and literally *drag* me away from the store window. I let that happen because he was just mirroring my thoughts about myself, which were: *You don't deserve to go in the store and try on the clothes, or even to* ***look*** *at them. You are not worth it.*

Mark had his own issues around money at that time as well, so we worked on this together. I said to him, "Buddy, what are you doing? I'm just looking and dream building. You're making me feel shit about what I deserve. You're being complicit in my negative money mindset, and I'm ready to let it go."

Of course, then I forgave him and myself, and looked at memories of my childhood to clear anywhere I felt unworthy of brand new clothes, or guilty for asking my mum to buy me something she couldn't afford. And there were plenty of those.

Step by step, I let myself go into the stores to look closer, and then gave myself permission to actually try on some new clothes. I gradually started to buy myself new things; but it was a process that didn't happen overnight. It took me *years* to stop shopping in second-hand stores, as I cleared and forgave old memories and beliefs.

I was in a thrift store recently, and while looking around, I noticed that I started to feel uncomfortable. I wasn't really enjoying being in there because all those feelings of unworthiness were coming back. I just wanted to go into a store where I could say, "This is my size, and I want it in red, black, and blue," and then just buy it if I liked it.

And again, this is a lifelong process. For example, even though I literally *am* rich these days, an interesting memory surfaced recently. I said to Mark, "Oh, let's not buy the beach umbrella from there – it's really expensive!"

His response blew my mind: "Denise, it's really not an expensive store, but I bet it was when you were a little kid."

Holy crap, he was right! It was a store that my mother would never buy things from, and she always tried to get us cheap imitations of the stuff we really wanted. I hadn't really cleared that, so I still perceived the store as "out of my price range." Fascinating, right?

I recently stepped it up a notch, and bought an expensive dress that was a little out of my comfort zone, in an area of the department store that I would normally have avoided as being "too expensive."

So yes, I'm still working on my own money blocks. *All the time.* But I seriously walk my talk, girlfriend, and there's always more to uncover. I'm always trying to increase my capacity for wealth, a tiny bit at a time, because I still have bigger money goals.

Sometimes when I'm shopping, I have to stop myself automatically going to the sale rack. Instead, I have to actually allow myself to try on clothes based on what I *like*, rather than what I think I can afford. You know when you look at the price tag before you really look at the dress to see if you like it? I'm breaking myself of that habit all the time.

Please note that I'd never suggest living beyond your means to pretend to be rich, or putting material doodads on your credit card to "act as if." You have to start where you are and just upgrade incrementally to the next step. If you always shop at Target, you're not going to buy your next outfit at Prada. It will feel energetically wrong (and it might not even be your taste anyway), so you'll find a way to sabotage it somehow.

Just choose the next step up. That way you won't freak out your ego. It takes time to truly and permanently increase your standards, and also to discover your true tastes when money isn't the only factor.

That's not to say there's something wrong with buying second-hand clothes or shopping at Target. It's all about how it makes you *feel*. If you love the thrill of seeking out and finding hidden treasures in vintage shops and second-hand stores, then absolutely keep doing it! If it makes you feel great to wear those beautiful vintage clothes, then go ahead.

For me it wasn't about wearing the clothes: it was about how the thrift shops made me *feel* – like I wasn't worth spending the extra money on to buy new clothes. But if you love it, by all means continue doing it.

> *"I like my money where I can see it, hanging in my closet."*
>
> CARRIE BRADSHAW IN *SEX AND THE CITY*

It sucks but it's true that women feel guilty more often than men. You rarely hear a man say, "I feel so guilty: I just had a piece of cake." We women, on the other hand, feel guilty about wanting things for ourselves instead of sacrificing our own needs for someone else. We feel guilty about wanting big dreams for our lives. We feel guilty about earning fabulous money.

I definitely felt guilty when I started my business because it started becoming really easy to make money doing what I loved. I still mostly work at home in my yoga clothes, and sometimes even in my pajamas (they are just *nicer* yoga clothes and pajamas than I used to own!)

I started this way when I earned my first $225, and it hasn't changed today. I've deliberately created a really chilled and relaxed lifestyle. Sometimes I'll work really long hours, and sometimes I'll just go off and see a movie. I have a nanny to help with childcare and laundry, a weekly house cleaner, and a meal delivery service. I'm not trying to be a superwoman, so I don't feel like I have to do everything myself.

People have said to me, "Oh, you're so naughty to go to the movies in the middle of the day" or "Wow, you're so lucky you have help!" When they do, I try to ignore that initial feeling of guilt, and instead make myself say, "No, this is how I've designed my life." It didn't happen by accident, and nobody gave me permission to do it.

I'm self-employed because that's how I want to live my life. I want to be able to go to the movies on a Tuesday afternoon if I want, and I'm not interested in cleaning my own house. Part of getting to live this way has been giving up the guilt of other people's opinions about what I should and shouldn't do with my money. Decluttering your old memories really helps with this!

> *"Money is the best deodorant."*
> ELIZABETH TAYLOR

My friend and mastermind buddy Leonie Dawson works just a few hours a day on her business, and has a multimillion-dollar turnover. When she gave up the expectation that she'd do what other people thought she *should* do, her business thrived.

She taught me her secret mantra... are you ready for it? It's "Fuk'em." Her philosophy is to be happy, and if other people criticize her for that, it's their problem. She also taught me how to delegate to my assistant, to not answer all my own emails, and to create some strong boundaries for my life.

But I had to forgive myself for wanting all of that, because I felt like a total diva bitch! I had to declutter memories of my family telling me, "You can't always get things your own way, Denise!"

As well as forgiving past business failures, forgive yourself for how you've handled money in the past – whether you have guilt from getting into debt, or from wasting money on a bad investment.

When I was twenty, I discovered this amazing thing called "Interest-Free Credit." I literally had no idea how it worked. (Hmmm, do you see the need for basic financial literacy classes in schools?) All I knew is that my friend went into this electronics store, answered a few questions, and walked out with a brand new laptop. Awesomeness!

So, I went back with three friends to get some of this "free" laptop action. There was no way I should have been approved for a loan on my student income, so when the salesman was filling out my application, he said, "Let's just say that your boyfriend pays your rent."

I was like, "Sweet! A new laptop *and* an imaginary boyfriend!" Twenty minutes later, I walked out with a brand new laptop... that I couldn't afford.

Well – you know how it goes. Once the interest-free part finishes, you always end up paying a ridiculous extra amount each month. Then I moved overseas and failed to make the payments, giving myself a terrible credit score. My mother had to pay off that loan; and the worst part was that the laptop got *stolen* a year later.

What a huge screw-up! So later on, when I was starting my business, I was still punishing myself with a crappy, slow Acer laptop, because I didn't feel like I could be trusted with a brand new Apple. I was still unconsciously punishing myself for that old mistake.

I could tell you many other stupid stories around my old money mistakes, but I'm sure you have a few of your own, right? Maybe more than a few.

These experiences from our past give us a framework through which we view our capacity to earn and keep money today. But by constantly doing forgiveness work on those memories, and by examining your past experiences in handling money, you can clear those feelings of unworthiness. And when you do, you'll give yourself permission to earn more.

Release family money drama

For some people, forgiveness work can be both a long process and a very intense time that opens up their eyes to the deep underlying issues they have around money. It can start to feel insurmountable, so if that's the case for you just do one forgiveness mantra – "I forgive you. Thank you. I'm sorry. And I love you" – at a time. It's only going to be ugly for a short time, as you're starting to clean out all the crap. And it will *never* be as intense as the first time you do it.

In fact, the intensity of the forgiveness work surprised one of my Bootcamp ladies, Victoria. She came from a comfortable, middle-class background, but when her family's business failed, they were forced to follow Victoria's father across the country in pursuit of money. So from an early age, she learned that money stresses people out and causes fights.

Her mom would tell her "Don't tell your father!" whenever she spent money, and would encourage her to lie about how much things cost. Who shares that memory too? I know I do! I also know that lots of women lie regularly to their husbands about how much they spend – even when it's their own money. Even when *they* are the breadwinner. Old family stories stick around: do you want your own daughters to repeat this behavior?

Victoria also married a man who had his own issues with money. Her husband always said he never wanted to feel like he didn't have enough money, because those times were so traumatic for him as a kid. Because of that, she kept all the finance matters hidden from him, so he'd never know when they were down to their last cent.

Instead, she carried the burden of their financial pressures on her own shoulders. She was stressed, and her husband stayed blissfully unaware; which – of course – meant that she resented him for it.

By doing her forgiveness work, Victoria realized it was not her husband's fault that she kept everything from him. That was just what she'd seen her own mother do. She was really forgiving herself *and* her mother for the past.

After doing her forgiveness work, another client – Natasha – said, "It just felt really good. Also, it reminded me that I'm human and that it's okay not to be perfect. What this exercise has shown me is that maybe I'm not so good with money, but there are one hundred and fifty things that my mother told me when I was growing up that have led to me having this particular attitude toward money. As long as I can identify those things and understand where they come from, then I can start working through them and letting them go."

It's not even your parents' fault. They learned their money beliefs from their parents, who learned them from theirs, and so on. Your mother learned to lie about prices from *her* mother... but you can break the cycle for yourself and your future family.

When Francesca – another Bootcamper – was young, her father passed away; and her stepdad's behavior caused her mother to go bankrupt. Francesca was switched on to the fact that this negative emotional experience could have an impact on both her own marriage and the way she dealt with her money as an adult. She did some forgiveness work around her experience, in an effort to move away from the fear that her husband would cause her financial and emotional distress.

"I have done a lot of healing around this, and now feel comfortable with having nice things and not worrying about the money too much – except for being responsible and paying my bills," Francesca said. However, some aspects of that experience still linger in her mind.

"My husband doesn't know that I have this secret savings account with money in it. I've always had this fear that I would end up making a lot of money, and I would end up with a dodgy husband like my stepdad who would take all of it," she said.

Although Francesca was partway there with her healing around this experience, she still had to go one step further. She had to forgive herself for her present actions, so she could have a healthy, adult relationship with her husband and their finances.

Hiding money from your partner through fear brings up some uncomfortable truths you might need to face. What are you afraid of? Why is this behavior happening? Is it something you saw your own parents do?

If so, clear it so it doesn't become *your* reality.

When forgiveness isn't enough

You can try many different treatments or techniques to help you break the pattern and release energy. I've done acupuncture, energy work, kinesiology, EFT (tapping),

Access Consciousness, Byron Katie's The Work, Brandon Bays' The Journey, meditation, Landmark Education, yoga – remember, it *all* works at some level.

So try different things to see what resonates with you and your belief system. There's nothing out there that's "better" than anything else; and you don't need fixing. You just need help clearing and decluttering old emotions. Try something and see. Don't get caught up in the method or trying to be "perfect."

As long as the message behind the methodology you choose comes back to self-love and acceptance, you'll heal yourself from the past. Avoid anything that will just add to your self-blame and shame, though. Gentle self-love beats self-punishment any day.

Dr. Masaru Emoto's famous book *The Hidden Messages in Water* is a fascinating example of how self-love can transform. He did experiments on vials of water by putting messages on them and thinking deliberate thoughts toward them. One vial label read "I hate you, I'm going to kill myself, I'm going to kill you."

Other bottles had positive messages, like "I love you." Researchers analyzed the water under microscopes to see if the different messages had different effects, and the results at a molecular level were astounding. The crystalline structures of the water with the negative messages were distorted, ugly, and irregular. The water with the beautiful, calming, and self-accepting messages had structures that were symmetrical, beautiful, and harmonious. This was at a microscopic level, but it was clear to see.

Again, I have no idea how that works, but holy crap! We consider ourselves so much more "alive" than water, so imagine what it does to our bodies when we give ourselves messages of self-hate, and run our low-level programs of negative thoughts or resentment. At a cellular level, we are creating negativity, lack, and distortion.

This is why the forgiveness exercises are so important: they have the power to change you at that cellular level, where you love and accept yourself, *no matter what.* When you do that, you can accept wealth into your life because you believe you deserve abundance at all levels.

> *"Everything we experience – no matter how unpleasant – comes into our lives to teach us something."*
>
> IYANLA VANZANT

Tammy Guest, one of my Money Bootcampers and friends, is a naturopath and she used Dr. Emoto's example to label her own herbal remedies. Instead of using words like "Headache" and "Infertility" on her bottles, she's created special labels infused with good intentions of "I'm well" and "I'm having a baby."

She tests her clients' blood before and after working with them, and she can literally see the effect that positive changes (including diet, exercise, meditation, positivity, and belief) have on their cells. It all contributes to an overall picture of wellness.

Seriously, you might be thinking, *what does this have to do with money?*

The answer is, *everything!* Money is just a symbol for your life. It's a symbol of how well you treat yourself. Imagine that your income is exactly proportional to your level of self-love. What does your current income say about that? What would it say about your ability to love yourself unconditionally?

When I see women setting and then failing to hit financial goals, I know it's got nothing to do with money, and everything to do with healing and forgiveness. So please don't be stubborn about it. Just freaking do what you need to do to heal yourself.

Book your session with the energy healer, get some therapy, see the doctor, do that EFT course, join my Money Bootcamp, etc. Whatever you decide to try, pay the money, and give yourself the gift of healing. Even if you don't feel anything is really "wrong," go deeper, and see what else you can uncover.

Heal your past lives

I'm not the most "woo-woo" person in the world – and trust me, I'm an extremely practical Virgo. However, in my quest to "throw everything at it," I also had an energetic clearing session with a past life expert. Jenny Hobby, an energetic healer, said that my poverty mentality came from at least 144 generations of my family, and she helped me to clear it.

Just thinking about how my money blocks could have come from my mother, from her mother, from her mother's mother, and so on, was incredibly powerful. Did we "really" clear them? Who cares?! It felt good; and it was a huge reminder to me about the impact I'll have on future generations.

I also had a past life session with Melissa Kitto of *Communicate with Angels*, who told me a fascinating story about one of my past lives. I was a Japanese artist and sculptor hundreds of years ago who refused to sell my art to the English – who were then coming to Japan in greater numbers. I was stubborn – wanting to be a purist and to sell only to local people – and fighting for the ideal of "Japanese art for Japanese people." This decision sabotaged my business to the point of bankruptcy, and ultimately caused a lot of shame for my family.

Now, whether or not you believe in past lives (I don't know whether I do either), that story provided a really clear message for me in my present life. It was an allegory for being stubborn to the point of not allowing my talents to shine for the greatest good. I could relate to that story, so I could forgive myself for past sabotages.

> *"People become really quite*
> *remarkable when they start believing*
> *that they can do things."*
> NORMAN VINCENT PEALE

Woo-woo stuff can be great for clearing old beliefs. Every meeting with an alternative therapy healer can be useful to reveal information about the habits that you need to change. At a recent acupuncture appointment, my practitioner asked me to tell him when the pain became too much.

Straight away, I steeled myself. I was going to withstand more pain than *anyone* else in his clinic. He was going to be so impressed! I caught myself in that moment, and it became valuable information about my stubbornness. When I told him about my awareness, he said, "Denise, this isn't a test. The treatment doesn't have to be painful to be effective."

I thought that was profound: healing doesn't have to be painful. It's just a tool so you can balance out what's not working and become more of yourself. And from a money point of view, when you give yourself permission to be perfect the way you are, you can become truly rich, both materially *and* spiritually.

When you accept and clear all of those old money memories, you will honestly experience a shift in your abundance that will astound you. No matter how crappy your childhood, and no matter how many times you've been cheated or ill-treated, it doesn't have to be your reality anymore.

You can transform hate and resentment into love and empathy. My guess is that you'll feel peaceful, happier, more productive, and more able to take action on your dreams.

And that's true wealth.

CHAPTER SUMMARY

❖ Forgiveness is the tool to release you from the past and allow you to be rich.

❖ No money memory is too big or too small to clear, and everything is symbolic.

❖ Throw everything at it – something will work and will free you from your negative self-beliefs around money.

Make sure you register for the book's bonus section at www.DeniseDT.com/Rich.

Chapter 5

What Do You Really Want?

*"All sins are forgiven once you
start making a lot of money."*

RuPaul

*C*an I ask you a personal question? We're friends now, so
you can tell me. I won't laugh at your answer, be shocked,
or think you're "too big for your boots." The Lucky Bee
community is an extremely safe space to share – and even
brag – about money. Here's the question: "How much do
you want to earn next year?"

That question might be easy for you, but it might also
make you want to put down this book and head to the
fridge. When most women are pressed, they can pull a big
number out of their butts. However, I usually either find that
their number is wayyyyy too small, or it's crazily unrealistic.

I've met women who have only ever earned a couple of thousand dollars in their businesses, whose very next goal is a million. I've also worked with women who just hope to earn the same amount of money as last year, and can't imagine how they could ever earn more. Whichever's true for you, you're in the right place.

This whole book is about getting you comfortable with earning more money, no matter what your starting point is. It's also about being comfortable with talking about money and shouting out loud to the Universe about *exactly* what you want in your life, no matter how simple or outrageous it is.

So that's why I asked about your income goal. You've got to get comfortable talking about it. You can't have goal shame and still expect to manifest your goal easily. I hear this all the time: "I'm almost embarrassed to tell you." Don't be embarrassed – it's only a goal. It's not a literal translation of your worth as a human being. (Spoiler alert – you're priceless!)

But it's time to get really clear with the Universe on what you'd like to earn, so it knows exactly what to deliver to you. Yes, you actually *can* put a price tag on that! No mixed messages and no goal shame.

Something happened when my first daughter was little that made me realize why women might be scared to set goals. It was my mother's birthday, and my two-year-old was helping to blow out the candles. We asked my mother what she'd wished for, and she said, "Oh, I can't tell you, or *it won't come true!*"

Then I noticed that Cinderella says the same thing at the start of the movie. Um. Wow. Did we really learn that from such a young age? That you can't say your dreams out loud because it will jinx them? That you have to hold it all deep inside, just in case? Mind blown.

I quickly said, "In our house, we talk about dreams all the time, so tell us what you wished for. It has *more* chance of coming true if you share it!"

Think about how many times you heard that as a child. Not only at your own birthday party, but at other people's, or when you wished upon the first star of the night. It's no wonder that goal setting – and talking about our goals – goes against the grain of what we believe.

The simple, everyday exercise that will change your life

This book is all about breaking old habits and beliefs, and Step 2 of the Money Manifesting Formula is all about learning to proudly state what you want.

Write Down Your Goals

The simplest way to manifest your goals is to write them down every day.

That includes your goal for *exactly* how much you want to make. It's a simple way to keep your goals top of mind; and the Universe will start to rearrange itself for you when it knows exactly what you want.

Many books, articles, and studies have been written on the power of goal setting. So listen to me and just do it, okay? (By the way, I say this to my husband all the time: "You know I'm right, so let's just pretend that we went through the resistance: now just do what I tell you to do." Yes, it's a dream being married to me, thanks for asking!)

Writing out your goals every day would be awesome. Every other day will create amazing things, and even just doing them once a week or month will put you so far ahead of the game it's not funny. Most people don't even write down their New Year's resolutions.

The act of writing your goals is important because it's a declaration that gets them out of your head and onto the paper. Plus, the intention behind writing them down actually requires you to think about what you want. Making that decision is the first step. I know it can sound really freaking obvious, and it may not be a huge revelation: *Write down your goals, that's your genius advice? I want my money back, Denise!*

Hey listen – I live and breathe this stuff, and I don't always remember to write down my goals every day. When I do, though, my money manifesting goes through the *roof*. Hearing it, and agreeing that it's important is one thing. Actually *doing* something about it makes all the difference though. It's almost 10 p.m. as I write this chapter, and I've yet to write down my goals today. So, I just took two minutes to write them. Simple.

You don't have to write them down perfectly every time: just doodle them down on a piece of paper. They don't have to be perfectly laminated either. They can change daily if you want, but the process of writing them regularly means that your most important goals will be revealed because you write them consistently. You'll probably start forgetting to write out your unimportant goals over time. If so, don't worry about them.

Don't be a perfectionist about this, or write and ask me to clarify exactly what to do. It doesn't matter. Write them in a pretty notebook, scrawl them on a beer mat, doodle them in your shower steam. It doesn't matter.

Nor does it really matter *how* you write them. You could do it in the present tense – for example: "I now have a successful business." Or you could write in the past tense, as if it's already done: "My business last year turned over six figures." You could even write in gratitude form: "I'm so grateful for my new $3,000 business idea." Don't worry about the how. Just *do* it.

Goal setting stimulates the part of your brain called the Reticular Activating System. This has two basic tasks: it controls mental alertness and also functions as a filter to categorize the most important information at any one time.

You can train your brain to choose what's important through regular and consistent goal setting. This will help you to recognize opportunities because it conditions you to actually *see* them. It's just like when you decide you want a particular model of new car, and then you see that model everywhere. Are there suddenly *more* of your dream cars on the road, or are you just training your brain to see them?

When you know exactly *what* you're working toward, you'll start to take more action toward achieving your goals because you'll train yourself over time to believe in them. Your belief fuels your action. Many "coincidences" and synchronicities will occur, and you'll see the *how* take care of itself. People will start to call *you* a lucky bitch.

> *"Don't simply dismiss a coincidence
> and let it drift away. Life is totally
> interconnected. These unusual 'things'
> are simply connections that surprise
> you because you aren't used to seeing
> life except in fragments. Now it is
> beginning to piece itself together."*
>
> DEEPAK CHOPRA

I heard once that the difference between a millionaire and a billionaire is that the billionaire writes their goals down *twice* a day. That quote lit a fire under my butt. So take two minutes now, and write down some goals. They don't have to be perfect. Just do it.

Remember Denise Austin, the 1980s fitness guru? Her slogan was *Do it every day, do it with Denise!* That's what I want you to remember. Goal setting needs to be an everyday thing if you want to manifest like a mofo. It's easy and it's free. Do it with Denise!

That's why you should always have your money tracking sheet to hand – either as a printed document, or open on your computer at all times. It will constantly remind you of your money goals, and how you're working toward them each and every day.

Your free Lucky Bitch money tracking sheets also have space for your monthly goals and current affirmation, but you must fill them out for the magic to work. Don't forget to download yours from the bonus section at www.DeniseDT .com/Rich.

When I was in my twenties, my goal was to be a millionaire by thirty. It had a nice ring to it, right? I know the reason I didn't hit that goal was that I had such massive unresolved lessons to learn. They meant that my twenties were less about money making and more about forgiveness, clearing, and decluttering my emotions, fears, and self-worth.

So my new goal became being a millionaire by thirty-five. One of my mentors, Ali Brown, was a millionaire by that age, so it seemed like a good goal. Someone I "knew" had done it. And I achieved it – actually a few months before my thirty-sixth birthday.

The key differences for the second goal were that I actually believed I could achieve it, *and* I had a plan to get it done. And honestly, the biggest difference was that I'd worked on my money blocks using this amazing set of tools that decluttered any fear or resistance I had to making it happen (which OMG, I had a *lot* of). Each time I increased my income, I went back to Step 1 of my Money Manifesting Formula, because – once again – there's *always* more to learn.

I want you to hear this though: I didn't do any "advanced strategies." I just did the same stuff you're reading about in this book – that which I teach on my Money Bootcamp. There's not going to be a second money book – *Get Richer, Lucky Bitchier* – in which I tell you the "real secret" to making a million dollars. *It would be the exact same book as this one!* Just "forgive more" or "Just do what I told you the first time."

So stop thinking that there's a silver bullet, or something else that you don't know, or a test you must pass to be "worthy." The basics work if you're consistent.

> *"Money is such an amazing teacher:*
> *What you choose to do with your*
> *money shows whether you are*
> *truly powerful or powerless."*
> Suze Orman

When I first ran my Money Bootcamp, I thought the information in it would only be valuable to women who were really struggling to earn good money. What I realized is that the lessons are the same at *every* level of income.

I was shocked to see women who were earning six figures, and were close to being millionaires, who still wanted to work on this stuff. For some reason, I thought that at some point, there'd be no more to learn. Big mistake. Let me say it again: there is *always* more to learn; and it doesn't mean that you're stupid, slow, or unworthy. It's just the journey.

So when women started joining my Bootcamp, it was interesting that even though they were all at different stages of wealth, they still all thought that the exercises were transformational... the *same* exercises. Some people were in crisis mode and were hearing it for the first time. Others just wanted to try out new techniques to go to the next level of abundance. The women who were already successful knew the power of goal setting, and knew that there's always more to learn about themselves.

And now that I'm in masterminds with other millionaire women, I see that they are working on the same mindset stuff too. They're still doing the basics – working on their blocks, setting new goals, etc.

At this point in your journey to getting rich, you might be starting to get frustrated if actual money hasn't shown up for you yet. After all, you've been decluttering like crazy, and you've set a massive goal... but nothing's shown up, and now you're like, "Where's my *cash*, mofo?"

Remember to keep tracking. Keep an eye out for symbols, like little coins or pictures of money. Notice, too, how much you get stuff for free. These are usually signs from the Universe that the money is on its way. But that could still leave you wondering, *Why hasn't it come?*

You might even be manifesting extra bills; this sucks when it happens, but trust me: it's happening for a reason. It's as though everything in your life that isn't aligned to money is bubbling up to the surface. All your past mistakes or bad habits around money are showing up.

This is exactly like when you start to take care of your skin, and you suddenly get a temporary breakout. You might think that it's a shitty reward for being so virtuous, but it's happening because you're uncovering all the crap under the surface. Don't give up – it's better out than in!

This temporary crap-fest or money drought can often be cured by *specificity*. Money *loves* clarity. The Universe is like the most loyal and enthusiastic dog in the world. It wants to serve you, but you've got to tell it what you want.

I saw a great documentary once about an incredibly well-trained dog that could identify thousands of different items. Her owner scattered at least one hundred different toys randomly around a live stage, and then asked the dog to fetch things: "Bring the parrot. Good girl! Now bring the rooster." This dog bounded around the stage to collect the items, and only got one thing wrong... out of one hundred. It was the most fun game ever for that dog: she loved being of service.

Now imagine that the Universe is like that dog. It's waiting there with tail wagging, expecting an instruction. As soon as you say the word, it will rush around, find what you want, and bring it to you.

It might not happen instantaneously. But the more you train the Universe to serve you, the faster it will happen. My six-month, all-expenses paid trip took six months to manifest, but I've also manifested large sums of money within 24 hours. My dream house on the beach took seven years and lots of "almost right" houses. When your manifesting muscles are well trained, it's *easy*; but it's not permanent. It requires daily action, which includes goal setting.

Back to the dog analogy. You don't train a dog to that level of obedience with just *one* training session, after which you give up because you don't feel like it anymore. It can take days, weeks, months, and even years of repetitive training, repetitive commands, and lots of positive reinforcement for the dog to learn different skills.

You also can't say to it, "Just bring me the *thing*. The *thing*. You know what I'm talking about. Surprise me."

Imagine the dog cocking its head and thinking, *What are you talking about?* **What do you want? Be specific**, and I'll bring it right now!"

So train the Universe by repeating your goals daily; and acknowledge the Universe by tracking your money daily. It could feel tedious and unrewarding at first, which is why most people aren't outrageously successful – they simply don't have the patience to continue. I've had many goals that I've abandoned because I wasn't willing to put in the work, so I just gave up. And by "work," I mean the daily commitment to making that goal happen on a practical and metaphysical level.

I told you I'd be honest and this sounds harsh, but not everyone is going to be rich. Most people say they *want* to be rich... but ask them their goals and they have no idea. Ask them to do forgiveness work, and they say it's too hard or unnecessary. "I tried that once and it didn't work," they'll say. Ask them ten things they could do to earn money right now, and they'll say, "I dunno. I can't think of anything." They'll just buy a lottery ticket instead.

Our community of Lucky Bees is different. We each take responsibility for our money. We're always looking for what we can do next, and we strive to get even clearer on what we want.

So when you're feeling frustrated, make sure you've given your money something really specific to flow to, and make sure you have at least one goal written down.

I have my lists scattered all over the place – in old diaries and on scrap paper – and it's fun to find them months or years later and realize that I can tick them off. Make sure you put a date on each list, so you can see how far you've come.

Remember: it doesn't have to be perfect. Just do it. Paper and ink are essentially free, so you're not wasting anything. And if you screw it up, start again. This isn't a one-shot deal. The sooner you define what you want, the quicker the Universe will deliver it to you. Trust me.

As you write down your goals, imagine that you have a magic pen and that everything you write on your paper with it is going to come true in the next six months. How cool would that be?

Sometimes when I'm doing this exercise at a workshop, I have people who sit there and stare into the distance, not knowing what they want. If that happens to you, just put your pen to the paper and see what comes out. Sometimes, if you just write one random thing, more ideas will flood to you. Don't overthink it – just write. What do you want to be doing, where do you want to be living, what do you want to have in your life over the next year?

Doing this exercise regularly always keeps your goals in the front of your mind. It's like creating a dream board but with words. Try not to limit or moderate yourself, even if your dream is to own a million-dollar house and you have *no* idea how it would happen. Dreaming is free.

Okay, let me tell you an awesome story about the power of dreaming – and why it's important to write your goals out regularly.

A few years ago, one of my goals was to buy a multimillion-dollar house overlooking the ocean. I wrote this on my goal list so many times, and I used all the tools I give you in this book. I even had the exact house picked out. I visited it all the time, pretending to drive up as if it were already mine.

I had a picture of it as my iPhone screensaver, and I used the street name as my password. The weird thing is that we knew the guy who bought the house next door. I felt like that was a sign from the Universe because suddenly, I was two steps removed from it.

I was starting to get impatient, so I made a tiny tweak to my goal – one that was entirely unintentional, but which changed my life. One day, I realized that I was writing, "**Live** in a multimillion-dollar house," rather than my usual, "**Buy** a multimillion-dollar house." Without realizing it, I sent a different intention into the Universe, which created a completely different chain of events.

You see, when you declare a big intention, the Universe sets off like that enthusiastic dog to fetch it for you. If your intention is a big goal, it requires lots of subtle changes to make it happen (imagine a complicated set of cogs and wheels working behind the scenes).

Although you don't see anything changing, things *do* move – even though it's slow at first. However, I'd been spending more time on the *how* than the *what*. I felt like it wouldn't "count" if we just rented a great house, but that was just a block I had to clear. I realized that I wanted the experience of living abundantly, and I really didn't care if I owned the house or not.

When I focused my attention instead on actually *living* in a multimillion-dollar house, my brain stopped worrying about house deposits, credit scores, and interest rates, and it came up with more creative solutions instead.

I realized that because interest rates were quite high at the time, it could be cheaper to rent than to buy. So Mark and I set out to find our dream house. It only took us six weeks from changing my intention and tweaking my goal setting to actually *living* in a million-dollar penthouse apartment overlooking the water.

The rent was about the same as the mortgage would have been on a house a quarter of its value. We didn't have to save for years, we didn't have to pay closing costs, and there was no long-term commitment. No, I didn't own the house, but I also didn't have to worry about repairs, rates, or market value either. For us, it was the ultimate instant gratification solution, and it came from changing just one word on my goal list. Powerful stuff!

Here's a really weird follow-up to this story. A few years later, we went to an open house inspection for a completely different house that we loved, but weren't in the position to buy. Guess who bought that house? The same guy who'd lived next door to our old dream house! But it felt like we were getting closer.

Fast-forward a few years and we bought a house in our dream street, just two doors up from the original dream house. I never lost sight of that goal and wrote it down for years before the money showed up.

It's actually *really* not uncommon to see *other* people manifest exactly what you want for yourself. That's why I wasn't too bothered that "our" houses were being "taken" by someone else. I knew it was just a sign that it was getting closer for us, and that the Universe was showing us that it was possible.

Remember, I'm not a financial advisor. I can't tell you to rent instead of buying a house. You also might have more patience than me, because I'm totally an instant gratification type of girl. But if you have a similar goal, then look around and see what's out there. Find out exactly how much it would cost to live in your dream house. Give up specifying the "how"s and just dream it.

This could actually apply to *any* of your goals. Whatever you want, you could get it much quicker than you think is possible if you're willing to change the rules about how you could get it, and open up to the Universe's creative possibilities.

I knew that I couldn't go to the next level of income in our first apartment. It was too small and old – my office was a tiny box room – and it was time to graduate from that place to something spectacular. The energy wouldn't have been right with my clients, even if they couldn't actually see where I was working.

It felt like a big, symbolic leap forward, and a massive upgrade. When we walked around the penthouse, I could see myself living there and growing my business. Mark kept trying to catch my eye to mouth, "Don't even think about it." But remember the story with the clothes shop?

This time, I mouthed back: "Trust me." And I made it happen.

The hilarious thing is that as soon as we made the decision to upgrade to the penthouse, my income practically doubled overnight. Even Mark's income increased. I had my best month ever after living in that apartment for just four weeks, and the following month was even better. We realized we could more than afford it when we looked at the actual price instead of daydreaming about it.

Since then, we've lived in lots of lovely houses, and trust me: it makes *such* a difference to your manifesting ability to be surrounded by beauty (more on that in the next step of the Manifesting Formula). And honestly, that simple goal-setting process sparked off everything. Being open to regular goal setting – and then tweaking the way I wrote my goals – changed everything.

Sometimes the Universe always has more creative ways to give you what you want. So don't get hung up on *how* you'll manifest your goals. Your job right now is just to clarify them and declutter any fears that surface.

Getting goal setting "right"

Remember that none of the dreams you write down are set in stone. You can always change them, or let them evolve over time. Having specific goals just trains the Universe to serve you.

Some women put off writing their goals (or taking *any* action) because of the fear of getting it wrong. One of my clients, Georgia, told me she procrastinated doing her list because she thought she only had one chance at it, and she didn't want to mess it up.

If this is the case for you, ask yourself what is the worst that could really happen. You use up a bit of paper – no big deal. Nobody's going to die. Even if you use your fanciest linen paper notebook and the most expensive fountain pen, it *still* doesn't matter if you screw it up. Just start again. I've completely messed up the first page in a new journal (terrifying for a Virgo) and just ripped it out and started again. No big deal – again, nobody died.

Like farts, goals are better out than in; so stop bottling them up and release them into the world!

Remember that the magic is in the *repetition*, not in how nice it's going to look on the paper. You don't have to laminate the paper; and perfect calligraphy won't manifest your goal quicker either.

Fears are also common when you try to set a bigger goal than normal. What will separate you from the average person is how quickly you recognize the fear, declutter it, and move on.

It's okay to work on your list over time – to refine it, perfect it, and change it. It will no doubt evolve as you work toward living your own version of a First-Class life. Remember that the difference between a millionaire and a billionaire is that the billionaire writes her goals down twice a day. So just do it. Now.

It's easy to justify to ourselves why we can't have what we want. We become fixated on *why* we can't have outrageous success, and we restrict ourselves to a little box. I've done it before myself too; but honestly, every reason you have for why you can't be rich is a BS excuse and nothing more.

I told myself that I couldn't be rich for all sorts of random reasons. I was too short (5ft 4in), not pretty enough, not skinny enough, not well educated enough, Australian, from a single parent family, a woman, I had a big butt...

Don't laugh: your excuses are probably pretty silly and irrational too! Too old, too young, too... something... You know who else is my height by the way? *Madonna.* But seriously, that was one of my excuses. If only I was a little taller... um. I call *bullshit.*

You can only make those big leaps in income by ripping apart the box that you've put yourself in (and yes, you're the only one who put yourself there). The label that says, "I can only earn this and no more" is self-imposed. If you think $100k is out of reach right now, or that you'll never reach a million, that's exactly what will happen. You don't need to know exactly how you'll get there right now. Just allow yourself to dream it and become a ruthless declutterer of every negative self-belief standing in your way.

Be aware of the labels you've put on yourself, thinking that you have to wait until you're the perfect weight, or more organized (or whatever), until you're "allowed" to be rich.

I recently had a Bootcamper tell me that she needed to take a writing course as her next step, despite the fact that she already had a really popular blog. Thousands of people read her blog every day; but she was self-conscious about her writing style, and *that* was why she couldn't make more money.

It wasn't true of course. She was just using it as an excuse. It was a minor distraction and a delaying tactic that we both recognized straight away. It was totally made-up crap.

Stop making excuses, and allow yourself to make money!

When I started my business, I remember thinking that I should get elocution lessons before I really became successful, just in case people didn't like my voice. Seriously. I even asked my coach about it, and she laughed at me. What a dumbshit excuse! It was definitely a creative procrastination tactic rather than a serious business strategy.

I've heard the same thing from many other women too though, especially if English isn't their first language. Spoiler alert – some people *won't* like your accent. But that's true no matter where you come from because it's statistically impossible that 100 percent of people will love everything you do. It doesn't matter though: it can only stop you making money if you *believe* that it will.

What excuses are you using? Give Yourself Permission to Be Rich Now.

Some women live their lives back to front. They want the money first, so they can *do* what they want. Then they'll *be* the person they've always wanted to be. They'll be happier, less worried, and – finally – perfect.

It actually works the other way around in reality. If you let yourself *be* who you already are, money will just enhance that. It will give you the freedom to *do* what you want and *have* anything your heart desires.

It's actually more important in the short term to *feel* rich, before you can be rich. Otherwise, how "rich" is rich enough to give yourself permission to feel good? How will you know when to stop accumulating money and start enjoying it? When are you allowed to be happy?

If I were to tell you my actual income right now, some of you would be impressed, some would be intimidated, and some would be like, *Is that all?* My barometer of financial success is that I *feel* rich: I have enough money to travel and live my life the way I want to; I keep the actual figure to myself. Yes, I earn a lot, *and* I'm still motivated to strive for new goals because I want to be a hell of a lot richer! You can aim to be better and still feel good about where you are now.

A few years ago, I went to Marie Forleo's Rich, Happy & Hot event in New York, where I was really inspired by the headline speaker.

A young woman came up to the microphone and said, "I'm doing really well in my business, but it's never enough. I grew up poor, and now I feel like I have to hustle all the time. I'm worried that I'll *never* be happy with what I've got."

The speaker's answer blew my mind: "Nothing will ever feed the poverty of your own soul."

Basically, his message was, "You're right. It will never be enough if you believe that." OMG.

Argh, so money won't make everything better?! Sorry, but no. Money is just a tool; and remember: money doesn't cure money blocks.

You have to decide *now* that you are enough. You are smart enough, pretty enough, clever enough, and ready enough. You can be richer starting today, if you're brave enough to define exactly what you want.

I find that my own income is rising rapidly now because I'm finally being true to who I am, and I know what I want. Honestly, money doesn't really define me; and I'm constantly surprised at how I'm a completely different rich person than I thought I would be. I'm pretty much exactly the same person inside, but I've become *more* of who I really am. It feels more authentic.

I used to try to be nice to everyone. (Remember my family motto: "It's nice to be important, but it's important to be nice.") When I started to become more of who I already was inside, not everyone loved it. My best friend broke up with me, saying, "You've changed and I don't like the person you've become." (Happy, fulfilled, on purpose...? *Okay.*)

I started being bolder in my messages on stage and in social media. Not because I thought it was "trendy," but because I'd actually been hiding before. Using the word "bitch" got me a lot of unfollows. I had a few people send me feedback that my occasional swearing bothered them, and that they didn't want to read my blog anymore. Yes, it hurt a little – but honestly, being more authentic felt better.

I didn't quite tell them to f-off, but I didn't worry too much about the feedback either. It was their opinion, and they could always find someone else to hang out with. I was sorry that they didn't like it, but they could always find heaps of other non-swearing books about money. (By the way, go check out my one-star reviews on Amazon if you want to feel good about your first hater!)

I had someone send me a lecture because I used the word "vagina" in a tweet. They said it wasn't professional, and that I'd probably lose followers. They framed it as very sensible advice that was in my best interests, and I *almost* took it on board.

Then I met S.J. Tierney, the author of *The Vagina Buffet*, one of my earliest coaching clients. Her book uses the word vagina about a million times, and it's awesome! (And by the way, "vagina" isn't a swear word!)

I had my chiropractor, a fifty-five-year-old man, tell me that I should change the name of my company because it implied that I felt I was better than everyone else. I almost took that on board too – even though he's pretty much the *opposite* of my target market. And why was I getting business advice from a chiropractor anyway? Perhaps it's because, like most people, when I was at the start of my journey, I was vulnerable to other people's opinions – on my goals, on my ability, and on my potential.

Many women don't trust that they can be wealthy without changing who they are. They think they'll have to "be better" somehow, and that's why they take advice (even completely unsolicited) from other people.

You might think you can't be successful and still be you. But again, *why not you?!*

Yes, even with all your "flaws." Why not you? Why can't you be the first? Nobody can tell you to change who you are inside, because that's where your wealth comes from. There's always going to be someone who loves you exactly as you are, and someone who hates everything about you (although not as many of those as you fear). The only thing you can do is be authentic to who *you* want to be.

Who do you want to be?

I've always wanted to be wealthy. I now know, however, that the reason I didn't hit my goal of being a millionaire by thirty is that I was trying to do things that weren't in alignment with who I am.

My first e-book was titled *Internet Dating Tips for Men* – and I was a little embarrassed about it. I didn't want to tell people about it, so of course it wasn't that successful. If I'd been passionate about it, I would've been happy to put more of my time and effort into promoting it, talking about it, and pitching it. Maybe then it would've been more of a success. But because it wasn't really "me," it died a slow death.

I spent most of my twenties doing a bunch of random jobs. I did a medical experiment to pay for my university tuition. I did commission-only sales in supermarkets. I did telesales. I even worked for a phone sex company for six months. I understand why I did it at the time – and back then I thought it was *hilarious* – but I'm sad now that I didn't believe I could use my talents in better ways for a paycheck.

The truth is that I'm a born leader and teacher. I've been doing this for a long time, but I've mostly been unpaid or underpaid. I had the skills to do what I'm doing now in my early twenties, but I just wasn't being true to myself. Because of that, I wasted my time in jobs that made me feel awful and didn't really bring in the big bucks that I wanted. Honestly, I didn't believe that I deserved those bucks.

If I'd followed my dreams and dedicated myself to being a coach, author, and mentor, I could've become a millionaire much earlier. (Okay, I know that thirty-five was still "young" to become a millionaire.) Honestly though, most of the lessons I had to learn have come with maturity and experience; and back then, I wasn't ready to do my forgiveness work. I didn't realize how many blocks I was living with every day.

If you're like most women, you really do know deep down what you want to do. It's probably always been there in your childhood – you just have emotional "stuff" in the way. When you clear that stuff, you give yourself permission to earn money in an easy, safe, and beautiful way.

I know now that money just enhances who you already are. You don't have to change yourself fundamentally to get it.

> *"If you're given a choice between money and sex appeal, take the money. As you get older, the money will become your sex appeal."*
>
> KATHERINE HEPBURN

Yep, it's safe for you to be rich and sexy!

Define what wealth really means to you

As you start to refine your goal list, you'll build a detailed picture of exactly what you really desire in your life. You'll see this happening *especially* as you do the decluttering work – because you'll give yourself permission to want what's truly important to you, instead of wanting your idea of what a "rich person" would have.

Being wealthy means very different things for different people. You might not want a Jaguar, or a BMW, or to even *be* a millionaire. You might just want to have peace of mind and to be happy. If so, that's cool.

But you still need to define what "peace of mind" actually looks like for you because it's too vague to be a useful goal. A goal like "I want more time" can't manifest – because everyone has the exact same amount of time in their day. The Universe can't give that to you, so it's a waste of goal-setting energy.

Let's break it down. Think about a goal like "I want to have more time with my kids." What does that look like to you? Do you just want to spend a whole day with them on Saturday, or do you literally want to spend all day, every day with them?

Think about what needs to happen for you to be able to spend an extra two hours a day with your kids. Maybe it means you need to get a cleaner, hire an assistant in your business, or have a certain amount of money coming in so the bills get paid without worry. Maybe you just want to be there for mealtimes or bedtimes. *Get specific.*

I set a goal one year to "have more fun" because I can easily become an anti-social hermit. But I knew I had to get more specific, so I came up with some simple things that sounded fun to me, such as:

+ Try pole dancing classes.

+ Make a dance video for my business.

+ Be involved in a flash mob.

+ Write a book about zombies.

Okay, I didn't do most of these, but they sounded "fun" to me. Drill down into all your vague goals so that they become more specific. This particularly applies to goals like "be less stressed" or "have peace of mind." Be specific, and choose just one thing that would cause you less stress, give you more peace of mind, or create more fun in your life. Just one thing.

> *"Money frees you from doing things you dislike. Since I dislike doing nearly everything, money is handy."*
>
> GROUCHO MARX

Maybe being wealthy means you can travel the world. Instead of just writing "travel the world" on your list, though, write down the places you want to visit. Maybe you want to spend a white Christmas drinking glühwein in Germany, or visit Japan when the cherry blossom is blooming, or go storm chasing in the USA during the hurricane season. (Personally, I want to swim with dolphins in Hawaii, wearing a mermaid tail.) Specific details like these will help to build your vision into reality.

Money is just a tool to help us get what we want

One of the most common things women put on their list is to be a good mother, daughter, or wife, and be happy in their relationships. (By the way, you can just decide *today* that you're good enough, or happy enough, and be done with it.) Getting those types of goal more concrete and clearly defined can be hard, but it can be done.

One of my earliest Bootcampers, writing coach Kris Emery, said she wanted to be a better daughter to her parents. That's a nice goal on the surface, but it's virtually useless from a Law of Attraction perspective – sorry Kris!

So I challenged her to get specific and measurable about it. For example, she could call her parents more regularly, or remember birthdays and send flowers. She realized, however, that she was holding herself back from what she really wanted to do.

"If I was really dreaming big and being honest with myself, I'd like to visit them more regularly. But I almost couldn't believe that would happen, so I didn't put 'a flight to the UK once a year' on my list," Kris said.

By setting this specific goal of flying home to visit her parents once a year, Kris had something positive to focus on and work toward. It's a much more concrete goal than her original one, and it's one that helps her to achieve her overall aim of being a better daughter.

Without being specific, you have kind of an impossible goal. How would you know you'd achieved it? Would you just always have this vague feeling of not being good enough?

Kris's goal also now has a numerical figure on it. She knows roughly how much a flight to the UK will cost each year, so now the Universe has something to work with. Instead of chasing a general desire to be "better," she can now feel good about achieving a weekly phone call and a flight home once a year.

If you still don't feel good enough after you achieve *your* specific goals, you can dig deeper into some of your excuses.

> *"Money isn't everything... but it ranks*
> *right up there with oxygen."*
>
> RITA DAVENPORT

You might feel resistance around doing this exercise – and that's completely normal! I believe the reluctance to take vague goals to the next level of specificity often comes from the fact that some goals sound nice in our heads, but feel like a drag in reality. Ask yourself how willing you are to make it happen in the real world.

For example, do you *really* want to call your parents every day, or spend *every* minute with your kids? Nope, probably not. Instead, pick something you can easily achieve so you feel like a winner. Otherwise, your goals become self-punishment. Achievement in little ways breeds more achievement in *big* ways, and money always follows good feelings.

You know that saying "you can't buy happiness"? Well, it's kind of true because "happiness" is a stupid, unquantifiable goal. You can buy a gorgeous teapot and fancy tea leaves that will make you feel happy for an afternoon. You can buy a new purse that will increase your happiness every time you use it.

You can buy an hour by yourself by hiring a babysitter, so you have time to do something that makes you feel happy. You can buy a day in a spa to feel relaxed. You can donate money to charity and feel good all day.

Money *can* create happiness, but happiness itself isn't a great goal because it's *way* too vague.

Unless you can state what you want as a SMART goal (Specific, Measurable, Achievable, Realistic, and Time-bound), forget it and let yourself off the hook. It's not necessary to be happy all the time to be an incredible manifestor. Strive for consistency, not perfection.

The Australian mattress company Forty Winks has a simple, shouty slogan: "Get a better bed!" It's short and to the point. Here's my version:

Get a better goal!

I'm just going to start randomly shouting that at people. No more Miss Nice Girl. If you tell me your goal is to be "happy," expect me to yell "Get a better goal!" at you.

Seriously, girlfriend: get a better freaking goal. You can decide to be happy right *now*. It's just not specific enough. Remember the dog that's ready to fetch stuff for you? What if the dog's version of happiness is to bring you the toy donkey? And then it sits there all confused, asking, "Why aren't you happy?! How can I make you happy?! Do you want the turtle or the parrot?!"

The Universe is the same: maybe you're getting sent all sorts of random stuff because you're just not getting specific enough. Get super specific about your goals, and the Universe will start arranging happy coincidences and synchronicities just for you, which is unbelievably awesome when it happens.

If your goals are looking a little flaky, define what you need to achieve them. For example "get fitter" turns into:

+ Be able to touch my toes.

+ Lose a dress size by June.

+ Be able to run on a treadmill for five minutes without stopping.

Think of these as mini goals that all add up to you attaining everything on your goal list or dream board. Plus, you'll feel like you're getting somewhere when you can actually define your progress.

Break down that useless goal like "peace of mind" into tiny bite-sized chunks, and the Universe will run to help you and fetch what you need.

How will you know? You'll find a pole dancing flyer in the mail. You'll see a sale for flights back home. You'll even start to see the money manifest to pay for it all. Why? Because you've given the money something *specific* to flow to. You've put a "price tag on happiness."

You can do this. Don't let your excuses derail your dreams.

Remember when you were a little girl? Think back to the first magical time that you blew out your birthday candles or you wished on a star. Take back the innocence and the belief that anything is possible. Because it is.

It's *your* time and you're ready for the next step.

CHAPTER SUMMARY

❖ Your money goal is just a number, not a literal translation of your self-worth.

❖ Money loves clarity, so define what wealth means to you.

❖ Goal setting trains your brain to look for opportunities – you can't screw it up or get it "perfect."

❖ Your excuses are total BS. But don't worry: everyone has them, so identify your biggest ones so you can clear them.

❖ The Universe is waiting for instructions, so get specific – otherwise you'll get random stuff.

❖ Get a better goal!

Chapter 6

Feel Good about your Money Now

"Stormy or sunny days, glorious or lonely nights, I maintain an attitude of gratitude. If I insist on being pessimistic, there is always tomorrow. Today I am blessed."

MAYA ANGELOU

Feeling good about your money is more important than the size of your bank account. However, that's not always easy when the reality is less than spectacular. You might not believe me right now, but that's okay.

I'm not going to lie. When you want to manifest a huge goal or break through to a new income level, sometimes you have to put in 150 percent. It's going to take a *lot* of mindset shifts to get there: you can't just write your goal down once and expect the Universe to completely rearrange itself for you.

Truth time: not everyone has the mental fortitude to continue through the temporary but highly inevitable bumps along the road to outrageous success. Sometimes this just seems like too much hard work, especially if you might not pull it off. Not everyone has the guts to keep going. Because trust me: it takes courage to be successful in life and business. Never forget how brave you are.

Now it's not *hard* work in the way that sweating down in the mines or becoming a meth dealer is. It does require a constant vigilance that the average person can't be bothered with, though. But I know you're different. I know how much you want to be richer, and I know that you're willing to study, learn, declutter, and put in the "work" to make it happen, no matter what.

When I was manifesting my six-month, all-expenses paid trip, I was super vigilant about my thoughts and actions. I really became the *ultimate* reverse paranoid, because – honestly – that's what it takes to manifest something out of the ordinary: total self-brainwashing. I had to live every part of my life as though I was about to go traveling on a great adventure. No room for doubt at all.

What would happen if you decided to feel great about your money *now*, no matter what your current reality? If you allowed yourself to feel rich *now*? This doesn't require super intelligence by the way. In fact, dumb, blissful ignorance would work best.

You just have to be willing to change your thoughts.

People email me all the time to tell me their stories of being broke. And although they think they're asking for solutions, they aren't really ready to hear any, because they're so invested in their current situation. They believe that they are broke, and they aren't willing to see their reality in any other way.

Some people want the Universe to shift and change for them, but they don't want to change their mental state *now* and believe something different can happen *today*. I'll tell them everything I'm telling you now: go and forgive every bad financial mistake you've ever made, find patterns to uncover your underlying beliefs around money, write out your goals, and then get more specific about them. Those people will just write back and say, "No, but how can I win the lottery?"

Sigh.

They don't need to win the lottery. Even if they did, they would honestly blow it all. The only shortcut is actually doing the work, and 99 percent of that is mindset work.

This is super, *super* important. You have to feel good about your money *now*, or you never will. If you don't try to feel wealthy now with what you have, you won't feel wealthy with 1 million dollars. You'll just feel this vague dissatisfaction, and then decide that if you just had 1.1 million dollars, *then* you'd be happy. Nope. Probably not.

That's why people who win the lottery usually lose it within five years. They aren't aligned to that level of wealth on the inside, and they haven't built up the energetic container to be able to deal with it. It's why the rich CEO works even harder and longer hours so he can get even richer. It's never enough. Remember: "Nothing will feed the poverty of your own soul."

This wealth game is a mindset one. And that can be the hardest kind of game, because nobody can solve the problem for you. Nothing external will "fix" it, not even more money.

> *"If everything was perfect, you would*
> *never learn and you would never grow."*
> BEYONCÉ

I know the feeling myself. Since I started in business, my income has grown dramatically, year on year. But that doesn't mean that all is perfect. My mindset challenges shift and change, but they're still there.

I have to remind myself that it's okay to feel safe and rich, no matter what. I have to be vigilant in my thoughts. Otherwise, no matter how much money I make, I don't feel rich.

That's why I recommend starting to practice now, because feeling rich starts with your everyday thoughts and feelings, which means that you can start today. Seriously – you've got to almost brainwash yourself with as much positivity as possible, and police yourself when it comes to verbalizing anything to the contrary.

Here's what Sandy Forster, author of *Wildly Wealthy Fast*, has to say about this: "Watch your self-talk. When you share publicly and use a lot of words like 'desperate,' 'don't know what to do,' 'scared,' 'give up,' etc., then what must you be saying to *yourself* in your head 24 hours a day? Your self-talk and your feelings are what you create."

Become conscious and very aware of what you're saying to yourself about money every single day – because that is your *order* for more of the same. When you shift your energy, your vibration, and your point of attraction, *everything* will change – believe me, I know it. I've lived it and I've transformed it. I know it's possible for *all of you* too!"

If you give up and start to go back to your old negative ways of thinking and speaking, your money manifesting will stop working. Mine does too. You'll be cosmically and financially constipated, and we know how that feels… awful! Whatever you're thinking, dreaming, or doing is what you're going to get back ten-fold.

I'm such an awesome manifestor now that I have to be extra careful about my thoughts, because I can manifest instantly when I'm in the zone. Things can *literally* show up almost instantly, so I have to be extremely vigilant.

That kind of manifesting power can be used for good or bad. As you'll discover for yourself, it's a double-edged sword. Luckily, you can learn to make positivity your default mood, so you manifest good stuff instead of more drama.

Remember though, I'm not perfect at this, and you don't need to be either. I'm just a normal person. I like to moan at my husband sometimes; I love reading columnist Lainey Gossip for the latest Hollywood gossip; and sometimes I have a bad day and just want to wallow in misery. But it doesn't last long because I know my income will be affected if I don't snap out of it quickly.

This doesn't mean you have to become a Pollyanna or a robot who isn't allowed to feel bad occasionally. You're allowed to have PMS. You're allowed to have an off-day – as long as you pick yourself up and get straight back on the Lucky Bee manifesting train as soon as possible.

The quickest way to feel rich now

Gratitude is the single greatest way to change your state from a feeling of poverty or lack, into one of feeling rich.

Mark and I always acknowledge every lucky thing that happens to us, even if it's a parking spot outside the shops. We'll say out loud, "Look at that, just for us! How lucky are we?"

In fact, being a Lucky Bitch isn't about being a bitch at all. And the lucky part isn't about bragging. Instead, it's totally about acknowledging your good fortune and feeling grateful for it.

Remember that tracking your income is a great start; and then, when you shift how you feel about it, you'll see amazing things happen. You'll attract more!

You might see that you've "only" manifested money on two days out of five. When you send gratitude to that experience, rather than blaming yourself, you're giving permission to the Universe to send you *more*. Say to yourself, *OMG, you clever Lucky Bee! That's awesome: I can't wait to see what you do next week!*

In the healing modality Access Consciousness, there's a magic question: "How can it get any better than this?" You don't ask it in a resigned or spoiled way, but with actual excitement and anticipation. Seriously, how can it get *even* better?

Another way to feel rich right now is to cultivate gratitude before you go to bed. Before I go to sleep, I love listing out the things I'm grateful for. That sends me off to sleep with a feeling of abundance and wealth.

Where's *your* hidden wealth that you're not even acknowledging?

When I first searched around for unclaimed money in my life, I realized that I had money accounts all over the place. I had superannuation accounts I'd completely forgotten about. I was holding myself back from claiming money from my US book sales because I was procrastinating over getting my US tax number.

It was going to cost me a couple of hundred dollars to get the tax sorted out, but the sales income was just sitting there, waiting for me to claim it! I had uncashed checks sitting in my wallet. I had unclaimed insurance forms. I had clients who owed me money. All of this unclaimed and unacknowledged abundance was just sitting around, waiting for me.

No wonder my manifesting ability felt stagnant. It was literally clogged with unclaimed money. So when you're feeling frustrated, look around and see what's holding up your goals, rather than making up stories about why the Universe doesn't like you.

Go on a Treasure Hunt!

Do you have more than one bank account with money sitting in it? You probably have a million unused gift vouchers (which are pretty much like cash). If you have accrued leave entitlements at work, calculate the dollar value of that.

Maybe some of your assets have increased in value – like your house, the value of your jewelry, or random collectables.

Go and collect all the money that is scattered through your car, clothes, home, and work desk. Trust me: you'll find a lot.

You might find a whole bunch of expired gift vouchers and pamper certificates (boo!), but you'll learn for next time, gorgeous (and some places will let you redeem them anyway). Remember: this is all abundance that you let go to waste. Is it any wonder that the Universe feels slow to deliver?

The last time I asked my Bootcampers about unclaimed income, these were some of the things they told me they'd found *that week*:

✦ Unclaimed tax rebate of $90.

✦ Reminder on a Post-it to remortgage house (saved $120/month).

✦ Costco refund of $120.

✦ A hair voucher worth $180.

✦ More than $13,000 in forgotten loans to family members.

✦ Loyalty card with free coffee ready to be claimed (worth $3.50).

✦ Enough frequent flyer points for a free flight.

✦ $300 hidden in an old book (seriously!)

✦ Unclaimed scratch cards and lottery tickets.

- Coins from old handbags – $83.45.

- Foreign currency in old travel wallets – $100.

- Fraud claim form for bank refund for $100.

- A book of forgotten stamps worth $25.

- A forgotten and unclaimed rental security deposit of $1,000.

- Amazon credit of $15.

- Forgotten PayPal money – $53.

- Uncashed checks from clients – $850.

You're literally surrounded with money that's just sitting there; and it's like the Universe is saying: "We've given it to you! Use it!"

Even people who are cynical about this eventually find something of value. Sometimes you have to do some belief decluttering in order for the money to unlock. For example, you might need to get rid of the belief that good things only happen to other people, and never to you.

It's so important to acknowledge and actually use every bit of cash and value that comes into your life. Here's why – just imagine that you have a goal of manifesting $5,000 every month. You're getting frustrated because you're only hitting $3,000. So you're like, "Dude, where's my money?" You start thinking that this Law of Attraction crap doesn't work for you, that you're a bad person, and that you're going to die a lonely and broke old maid. *Thanks, Denise!*

But the Universe *is* giving it to you, if you pay close attention. Round up all those hidden opportunities, and I bet you hit your goal every time.

Automate your positive feelings

I'm the laziest person in the world. Seriously, my next book should be called *Lazy Bitch* because I always find the shortcut. Things have to be really easy for me if they're going to stick. I rarely remember to take vitamins, going to the gym is a drag for me, and I outsource *everything* because I can't be bothered doing it myself.

In my book *Lucky Bitch*, I shared that in my first telemarketing job, I refused to actually telemarket – because it was so painful. We were given a giant list of people to call, but I made fewer than ten cold calls in the two months that I worked there. Yet I was the number two salesperson in the company and made great commission. How did that happen?

I got bored making calls, and the odds of actually making a sale doing it that way were so low. It was the world's most demotivating job, but I needed the money. So one night, I tried an experiment: when everyone else went home at 9 p.m., I stayed an extra hour, to see how many potential customers would call in, wanting to sign up after hours.

It turned out that there were a lot. Normally, they would hear an automated message asking them to call back within office hours, but these were motivated customers, and guess who was there to take the calls? Me!

In time, this shortcut was enough to make me number two salesperson. Yes, I had to work an extra hour for free, but the commission made up for it. Plus, I didn't have to do the painful work of making cold calls during my work hours. (Honestly, I kind of messed around during that time, but my bosses didn't care because the results were so impressive.)

So I'm a big fan of finding easy shortcuts for the Law of Attraction to work for you.

One extremely easy and automatic way to keep your vibration high is to build your desires into your everyday environment. This is my single greatest manifestation tip. Because you don't have to think about it, there's absolutely no willpower or effort required.

What are your passwords for your computer, your phone, and your online banking? Are they something completely random, or do they excite you every time you type them in? Typing them is something you do anyway, each and every day, at least ten times; so make them something like "6figures," which was my laptop password for a year until I hit my goal.

After that, it became "7figures." I honestly didn't believe I could hit a million dollars in my business at first; but typing it in every day, multiple times, helped me to believe it.

When I told my mastermind buddies my big goal for *this* year, they asked me what my plan was. I said that the first thing I'd do would be to change my password. Obviously that isn't all I'll do, but it's a great start! So if you've hit your goal, don't forget to change your password!

What are you choosing for your bank account names? Some banks allow you to change the name of your account as it's displayed online. So you could have a "savings account" or a "savings for house," but you could also change it to be anything. Rather than having an account called "Debt," why not name it your "You Can Be Financially Free" account or your "Hawaii Holiday"?

My savings account is called "Money Loves Me." Every time I put money in there, I'm reminded of my mantra

"Money loves me and takes care of me." My expenses and receipts folder in my email account is also called "Money Loves Me." Who knows how often I actually see it, but it's there, casting a subtle subliminal spell. Every little bit helps.

Set up automatic reminders on your phone with pop-up messages. There are apps, or you can do this under your calendar or reminders, and set them as recurring events. When I was writing my book proposal, I had "Congratulations on selling a million copies of your book. You're a publishing success story!" popping up every day, which encouraged me to keep going. When we were looking for a new house, it was "Million-dollar beach house is yours!"

Yours could say, "Remember: you're beautiful!" or "Way to go on breaking six figures this year!" They'll pop up out of the blue, and when they do, take a second or two out of your day to think, *Hell yeah!* It's getting into the *feeling* of these reminders being true that makes them so powerful.

You can go crazy with these little messages so that they are infusing your conscious and subconscious mind every single day. Make it so that you literally can't go an hour without at least a small reminder of your goals. It will make a huge difference.

Here are some of my best lazy manifesting tips:

✦ Listen to subliminal meditation CDs with messages about abundance and wealth as you work.

✦ Put Post-its around the house with your goals written on them in the present tense.

✦ Read or listen to the autobiographies of wealthy women on your commute.

- Display your dream board where you can see it (printed out, on your computer desktop, and on your phone).

- Doodle pictures of your goals when you're on the phone, or gaze at your dream board when you're on hold.

- Listen to motivational CDs in your car, so that as soon as you turn on the ignition, you're immediately back in the zone.

- Laminate a goal list for your shower.

- Write your biggest goal in the shower steam each morning (I draw hearts and dollar signs every day).

- Put your goal list on the back of the toilet door: may as well use that time well!

- Keep a notebook in your purse, so you can re-write your goal list when you're in a waiting room.

- Sign up for Notes from the Universe at Tut.com.

- Get my weekly newsletter at www.DeniseDT.com /newsletter.

- Use novelty money items, like napkins printed with dollar bills.

- Keep $100 in your wallet and never spend it – just look at it daily to make yourself feel abundant.

- Put a tiny goal list in the window portion of your wallet where you'd normally put your license.

- Get a personalized number plate – mine says LUCKYB.

- Make a money-related playlist on iTunes.

✦ Watch TV shows about money and rich people (and if it triggers you, then it's great info to clear and release).

✦ Set up an automatic savings account, so you have a rainy-day fund.

One of my favorite secret success tools is subliminal learning affirmations. I use them for everything: creativity, relaxation, self-love, *and* abundance. Subliminal means "below the threshold," which means that the messages are just below your conscious perception. They can activate specific regions of your brain without you being consciously aware of it, but your unconscious mind still hears the message.

Affirmations work beautifully, but you're not going to sit there for hours repeating them to yourself. Who has the time or the willpower? No, hearing them recorded with beautiful music over the top is an excellent (and lazy) alternative that's much more practical for the average person.

Listening to subliminal meditation tapes has definitely worked for me, so I think it's worth trying. Some people say that it works entirely because of a placebo effect (i.e. because you *believe* it will work), but that's fine by me. Remember: throw everything at it.

I listened to my first subliminal meditation tape in high school, when I was studying for my final exams (it was one about having a good memory). Then I listened to one when I was writing my first book (with messages about creativity); and then finally, I created my own: all about money, wealth, abundance, and success.

My Money Bootcampers get my special Money Mantras subliminal meditation as a free bonus; and even I was astounded at how well that worked! For this meditation,

I recorded 1,111 mantras and affirmations about money, and then put a soundtrack of relaxing beach sounds over the top.

You can't actually hear the affirmations consciously (unless you listen really, *really* hard), but the message goes into your subconscious in a powerful way. You can just play it in the background of whatever you're doing, even when you're asleep (just not while operating heavy machinery). No effort required. Within a few days of sending it out to my Bootcamp peeps, I started to get all these random emails about crazy money manifestations.

The point is – *everything helps*. If you want a free five-minute version of the Money Mantras subliminal CD, you can claim yours in the bonus section at www.DeniseDT.com/Rich.

Will your goals into existence

When I was in the process of writing my first book, *Lucky Bitch*, I still wasn't confident in myself as an author. So I changed my email signature to "Denise Duffield-Thomas – Coach and Author."

This might not seem like a big deal, but I didn't yet believe that I was a coach or an author. I felt like I was pretending by changing my signature. Then, as I wrote my book, I saw that signature every day – and it reminded me that I was definitely in the process of becoming an author (even though I had trouble telling people about it).

Plus, even though I'd done my coach training, I wasn't ready to claim being a coach either. That meant it was difficult for me to make money from coaching. It was a tiny little thing, but seeing that signature multiple times every day gave me confidence. Other people saw it, and they believed I was both of those things. Their belief strengthened my own, which *willed* it into reality.

After a few weeks, I changed my signature to "Author of *Lucky Bitch*," which gave me the confidence to finish my first book. It helped me step into an energetic space where I *was* that person. Every time I saw it, I believed in myself just a tiny bit more.

The same is true when you create account names for online forums or Twitter. Be aware of the energy you're putting out there. It's a bit of a pet hate of mine when people don't put their name on their account, and instead use a nickname. Bootcamper Kris Emery once used @sohighlystrung as her Twitter name, but has since changed it to reflect her copywriting business name, @KrisEdits. Much better energy, right? Good work, Kris!

Seriously, Denise, does all this stuff really make a difference? Aren't you going a bit overboard?

No. Words have power. Everything has significance. Every action you take has significance to your self-worth – and inevitably, your net worth. All these things might seem random, but it all compounds over time to increase your wealth consciousness.

So next time you're online, change your signature, your passwords, and the names of all your accounts. Ensure that they're exactly what you want them to be, not something random and without meaning. Really look and see what you're putting out to the Universe.

These things are easy changes to make, and require very little thought or effort on your part. It's the lazy girl's guide to manifesting!

Every time you see one of your automatic reminders, or type your goal instead of a password, it's another message to your subconscious that you're ready for your goals to manifest, and that you're ready to claim being a wealthy woman.

Crowd out the negativity

When you want to make dietary changes, it's easier to simply crowd out bad food with healthier options, rather than making massive changes that ending up sabotaging your diet. It's the easiest way to make a behavior change. Anything else feels too hard.

All of the easy actions in the previous sections of this book compound over time; and the idea is that all the positive messages about money will crowd out the negative. It's really the lazy person's manifesting tool bag.

Another thing to watch is what you put out into the world. Be aware of the energy you put out on social media: the words and phrases you use. And seriously, please don't spread urban myths and fear-based messages without researching if they are actually true – they create fear for everyone and are a complete waste of time and energy.

Only spread positive messages. (This doesn't mean you can't be an activist or stand up for what you believe in, just be discerning and use your energy wisely: you can't fight every fight in the world.)

When I'm having a bad day, I stay away from social media. I'm aware of my growing audience, and I wouldn't want to infect anyone with my (temporary) negativity. Sure, I'll share real-life struggles to show that I'm not perfect either; but I see my job as inspiring people, not being a Denise Downer.

Besides, if I share it, I'll stay in that negative state longer – and I want to get out as quickly as possible.

You'll never hear me say things like "It's so hard to get clients/make money/get out of debt!" or use language like "desperate," "broke," "scared," etc. I don't complain about taxes, the government, or the price of things either. I rarely go on negative rants (except occasionally something weird and Virgo-related, like how nobody knows how to hang clothes for optimal drying time, or how to stack the dishwasher properly) because that will infect my day too.

If I see too many negative messages from a friend, client, or family member, I'll actively hide them from my news feed. And really negative people? I'll unfriend them. Either way, I have to protect myself and my energy – and so do you.

I choose the news I want to watch, and avoid most forms of sensationalist media. I don't watch much horror anymore (except the occasional zombie show), and I sidestep any political or religious discussions that might raise my blood pressure. It's not worth it.

I've also phased out friendships with people who invite too much drama into their lives, who use more negative than positive language, or who constantly obsess about their problems without doing anything about them.

Honestly, it's okay to say no and ban people from your life if they aren't adding to it in a positive way. Basically, *you can choose*. You choose the messages you take into your brain.

I'd say more on this topic, but my friend and mentor Leonie Dawson says it better. I've quoted below a section from her book *73 Lessons Every Goddess Must Know* – with her permission of course:

You Have Permission

by Leonie Dawson

Dearest Goddess,

Today, and every day, you have permission.

You have permission.

Today, and every day, you have permission.

You have permission to say no to demands on your time that don't light you up, and don't give energy back to you.

You have permission to not give a crap what's happening outside your world, and keep your energy focused on what you're creating.

You have permission to let go of friendships that make you feel like shit.

You have permission to say no whenever you like, however you like, in whatever kind of voice you like, without feeling like only Mean Girls Say No and Nice Girls Say Yes. That's bull. Yes and No have equal weighting – what's important is if you use them when they are the best thing for you – not out of fear, obligation or guilt.

You have permission to know that Yes is powerful, and so is No. The power comes from you using either from your highest spirit and truest integrity.

You have permission to change. You have permission to not be the person you once were.

You have permission to get angry and self-righteous, and to also glean the wisdom from those emotions.

They are leading you to where your boundaries are, and where they have been crossed, and what you need to do from now on.

You have permission to be exactly how you are.

You have permission to not be more like anyone else in the world, even if you think they are better, wiser, or more popular. You have permission to be more like yourself, your gifts, and your wisdom.

You have permission to not care what other people think of you.

You have permission to not try to change what other people think of you. You can't ever argue that you are a good person. They will either know you are, or not. You don't need to spend time with people who don't believe in you.

You have permission to do things that your friends and family do not.

You have permission to be wild, expressive, truthful, exciting, and outspoken.

You have permission to not accept friendship requests on Facebook, or anywhere else in your life. You have permission to block people whenever you like.

You have permission to share as much or as little as you like. You have permission to blog, or not blog. You have permission to Twitter, or not to Twitter. It doesn't really matter. As long as it's making you happy, that's the best thing.

You have permission to suck at a wide variety of activities. It's okay. You make up for it with your million other brilliance particles.

You have permission to be whatever body shape you like.

You have permission to choose, and choose again. And then choose again.

You have permission to not always be a perfect image of something.

You have permission to be a contradiction.

You have permission to not go to your school reunion, unless it really excites you and delights you, and you would love to really heart-reconnect with people you went to school with.

You have permission to not be interested in the newest fad: harem pants, geek glasses, Polaroid cameras, scrapbooking, macramé. You also have permission to be totally obsessed with them, if it makes your heart light up.

You have permission to cut people from your life. You have permission to surround yourself with people who are good and loving and nurturing to you.

You have permission to be a disappointment to some people, as long as you're not a disappointment to yourself.

You have permission to do nothing whenever you like.

You have permission to make your big dream come true.

You have permission to not do it all perfectly, or have all your shit together.

You have permission to not forgive people. You have permission to forgive people when it's right for you.

You have permission to think some people are crazy. You have permission to think some people are smigging ice-cream with chocolate and wafers and sprinkles and cherries on top.

You have permission to not have the perfect relationship.

You have permission to not have a relationship.

You have permission to take whatever time you need for you.

You have permission to make ridiculous choices for yourself.

You have permission to use and listen to your intuition. To feel when things are off, and to remove yourself from them, even when you don't quite know why. You'll always find out why. Our intuition is here to serve us.

You have permission to be down. You have permission to be up.

You have permission to still believe in unicorns and fairies.

You have permission to believe in things that other people think are very, very odd and strange. You have permission to not care. You have permission to believe in things that make your life wholer, richer, and deeper. You have permission to make your own world that is the truest painting of you.

You have permission to suck at coloring in.

You have permission to say bugger off to anyone who has ever told you that you're not good enough, you're not worth it, you are not beautiful, you are not lovable and you are not the most divine, wise, delicious Goddess to walk the planet.

You have permission to know that you are.

You have permission to swear when you like, however you like, to your reckless abandon.

You have permission to not be the best of anything – just the best of yourself. And some days, just the best you can do that day.

You have permission to not always give. You have permission to fill your own cup up first.

You have permission to have things around you that delight you.

You have permission to live in a tipi if you want to, or a mansion. Whatever makes your spirit shine is the right thing for you.

You have permission to make choices on whether it makes your spirit shine.

You have permission to know you are a goddess, even when it doesn't feel like it. Even when you feel utterly human. Even when you want nothing more than to climb under your blanket, or light up the sky.

You are a goddess.

You have permission.

You have permission.

You have permission.

Big love, Leonie

You can find the gorgeous Leonie at www.LeonieDawson .com.

CHAPTER SUMMARY

❖ It's going to take more mindset work than you think, but it's worth it.

❖ You are richer than you think you are.

❖ Watch your thoughts about money all the time. Be vigilant, and protect yourself from negative money thoughts.

❖ Gratitude is the quickest way to feel rich now; and when you feel rich, you'll attract more money.

❖ Money is all around you, so open up your eyes and go on a treasure hunt.

❖ Crowd out the negativity with as many positive messages as possible. You can't overdose on the good stuff.

Bonus – get your free Money Mantras subliminal meditation at www.DeniseDT.com/Rich.

Chapter 7

Upgrade Your Life Now

*"Little changes and little choices add up to
be revolutionary changes in your life."*

SARAH BAN BREATHNACH

I believe in making quantum jumps in success; but sometimes moving forward even a tiny bit will help, especially when you're feeling blocked around money.

When you live a life of constant but incremental upgrade, you *will* attract more money into your life. Teeny tiny amounts at first, and then more and more. The speed and amount of money totally depends on your bravery and willingness to push yourself further.

One really common thing that I hear from women all the time is: "I can't wait until I'm rich." And then they talk about all the things they will buy "when" they're finally rich.

My husband Mark and I used to have that conversation *all the time*, thinking that we were acting "as if" we were going to be rich. In reality though, we were pushing the time when we'd be rich further away to "one day."

It was exactly like when we were dating. Friends and family would ask us when we were getting married, and for *years*, Mark would answer, "In two or three years."

Finally, I told him, "Buddy, you know that has to start counting down, right? It has to be two years, then one year, and then eventually you have to actually produce a ring. Like *now*."

You can't be rich *one day*. You have to start today. Yes, it's fun to speculate about the future, but do you know what's even *more fun*? Actually *living* it. You can't rely on someone else to make you rich. I know, because I tried. I thought that Mark would be the stable breadwinner, and that my money would come "some day." It didn't.

When we were first dating, I earned more than him (he was a student). Then he started out-earning me at work, while I got overlooked for promotions and pay increases (because honestly, I didn't believe I deserved to earn more).

It sucked at first – because I was the one reading all the money books, going to wealth development seminars, and investing in coaching. It wasn't until I worked on my money mindset, and upgraded my life without waiting for anyone else to "give it" to me, that my income took off.

I keep on talking about the "real world," as opposed to the one in our heads. It's so easy to live in a state of "what if" when you're reading inspiring wealth books. We can all imagine what we'd do with a million bucks without much trouble, but ask us to pay for an upgrade before we feel "ready"? No way!

> *"Life shrinks or expands in
> proportion to one's courage."*
>
> ANAÏS NIN

Please know that I'm *not* talking about going into credit card debt, or spending money you don't have. Spending money just to impress other people also doesn't work. If overspending is your sabotage pattern, spending more isn't going to fix anything. You're not necessarily going to feel rich just by buying expensive things (especially if you can't afford to maintain them), unless it's a conscious choice that makes you feel really good about yourself.

One of our Bootcamp members, Debbie, admitted she had a problem with spending. In her own words, she would "spend money like an alcoholic would drink." She would do it in secret, and then feel awful about it later. She was addicted to spending, but not on things of value that improved her life. She was spending for the sake of spending: a classic sabotage.

To stop this sabotaging behavior, Debbie made the decision that her bank account was never going to go to zero. Instead of trying to stop herself spending "cold turkey," she created a new "energetic overdraft limit" that was just a few hundred dollars to start with.

As long as she had a positive bank balance, she allowed herself to keep spending; but she slowly weaned herself off the urge to spend until she had nothing left. Then, over time, she gradually increased that "overdraft limit," until she was comfortable having several thousand dollars in her account. In other words, she created a new energetic comfort level.

If you're in a lot of debt right now, this book will help you work on some of the mindset blocks that got you there in the first place. As you clear those blocks, you might find yourself wanting to follow Debbie's example, or even wanting to go cold turkey by cutting up all your credit cards. Again, remember: I'm not a financial advisor, so I can't tell you what the right real-world actions are for you.

I can tell you though that when I first started working on my money mindset, I got rid of my credit card; instead, I experienced the pleasure of paying for things with cash. I paid for my laser eye surgery in cash (literally – with fifty $100 bills). You bet *that* made me feel rich. I bought my car in cash (again, literally), and owning that car outright felt amazing at the time.

You don't always have to spend a lot of money to feel rich. Before the actual money showed up, I started doing things every day that made me feel rich and cost nothing. They were things like wearing my favorite perfume, doing my hair, and actually *using* some of my "for best" items like china or the teabags I'd always saved for guests.

When I felt rich, I acted rich, which then gave me the courage to change more things in my life. Buying things on credit cards didn't really make me feel rich (beyond the momentary thrill I got). Instead, they made me feel trapped in a cycle of debt.

When you find the things that make you feel really rich deep down inside, they will help you to act in more positive ways to attract more money.

It's a beautiful virtuous cycle.

In this chapter, you'll be inspired to put your money in places that might make you feel uncomfortable, and your comfort level around each expenditure will be completely personal to you. You might be totally okay with spending money on organic food, but wear the grubbiest underwear known to womankind. You might be totally comfortable staying in five-star hotels, but the thought of saving even the tiniest amount of money each month scares the shit out of you. It's okay. It doesn't matter what your particular money "problem" or sabotage is, the way to solve it is by making tiny upgrades.

It might seem crazy at first to spend money on yourself or live more extravagantly than you're used to. However, by making minor upgrades, you'll to start to vibrate at a higher frequency of wealth – because you'll feel the joy and satisfaction of having or doing those things *in the real world*. And guess what? Yes – you guessed it – that means you'll attract more positive vibrations, so your money manifesting will become easier and more powerful.

Let's change the conversation from "I can't wait" to "I'm so lucky" and "This is so much fun!" We'll upgrade your life in such clever, sneaky ways that your favorite forms of sabotage won't even have a chance. Yes, you might have momentary freak-outs, but you'll also have the tools to deal with them. It just becomes a fun game – what can you upgrade in your life next?

When you start making minor upgrades to your life, you essentially build and grow the power of your manifesting muscle.

The law of incremental upgrade

I embraced this concept because I was fed up with my constant backsliding after the hype wore off from yet another money book or personal development seminar. I was initially excited and *pumped* to the max; but I had no idea what to do with the information I'd learned to actually make concrete changes in my life. Everything seemed so overwhelming.

I wanted to live in a beautiful beach mansion by the sea, have an amazing car, wear gorgeous clothes (that actually fit properly and didn't smell of a thrift shop), have nice hair, and be surrounded by wealth, ease, and beauty. I wanted to make a teleporting leap out of my current life into something amazing, and have everything change in an *instant*. Honestly, I wanted to win the lottery but not change myself from the inside.

I was totally on board with the "millionaire mindset," but the *reality* of my life didn't match it. I looked around at our small apartment, in literally the only area we could afford. I looked at the house itself: so wonkily built that all the furniture slanted in different directions. And I realized that *everything* in my life was make-do.

I had so many workarounds to make it through the day. You know when you don't even realize what you're putting up with, until you have someone come to stay and you say, "Oh, the shower works if you jiggle it a bit and then crank the handle five times." Virtually everything in my life was like that. I remember the time our cheap Ikea bed broke, and I spent a whole Saturday constructing an elaborate fix out of plywood and glue because we couldn't afford to buy a new bed.

Everything in my life was cheap, cheap, cheap... but I felt paralyzed to do anything about it. I didn't have the money to fix anything, and I felt stuck. There was *too much crap* to handle all at once, but I put pressure on myself to suddenly become this rich chick overnight. Even if I got a windfall or pay increase though, nothing really changed and the money left quickly. I wasn't energetically *aligned* to wealth because my overwhelming experience was mediocrity and a "make-do" mindset.

Let me be clear here – the way I experienced poverty in that time of my life wasn't poverty as we know it on a global scale. I understand that. My "shitty" life and wonky apartment was someone else's idea of extreme wealth. I don't think it's fair that people starve or die needlessly from diseases, and I'm not being insensitive to that. However, this isn't a book about global economic justice (yes, that is an incredibly important topic, but it's not my area of expertise). This is a book about removing all the obstacles from you being as wealthy as you want to be, regardless of where you're starting out.

The ironic thing is that when you commit only to making incremental upgrades, you can actually make the quantum leaps much quicker. That happens because you build a strong energetic foundation, so you're less likely to sabotage your success. This simple process of incremental upgrades has changed my life, increased my income, and *finally* allowed me to feel rich.

Create your upgrade plan

An upgrade plan isn't rocket science, so don't overthink it. Just follow this really easy process to start making incremental upgrades in your own life:

1. Think about what makes you feel poor.
2. Pick one thing to upgrade.
3. Repeat.

Let's break the process down a little:

1. *Think about what makes you feel poor*

This is your reality moment – where you see how you're *really* treating yourself, and what you're *really* putting up with.

Write down everything in your life that you'll no longer put up with "when you're rich." Anything that annoys you, embarrasses you, or makes you feel poor.

For example, you might think that the "rich person" version of you always wears perfume. In reality, however, you never really believe you deserve it, so you wear your cheapest stuff every day. Or you use a broken teacup while your beautiful one collects dust on the shelf.

2. Upgrade

The next step is to simply pick *one thing* at a time, and upgrade it to the very next level. Just a teeny tiny bit, so you don't freak out.

If you really can't bring yourself to spend more money, or things feel really tight right now, you can start by wearing your favorite clothes more often. You could also wear your most awesome shoes, use all the beauty products in the bottom drawer, use your perfume every day, or give yourself some extra minutes to do your hair and makeup. Those are all free, but they'll make you feel amazing. If you don't take the time now, what makes you think you'll start doing it when you have more money?

Allow yourself to use your best bed linen more often; or better still, go out and buy gorgeous Egyptian cotton sheets that make your bed a real oasis of calmness and a special place to rest your head. You'll go to bed feeling richer, and wake up feeling richer. Imagine what you can achieve with that kind of confidence.

Or imagine that your *idea* of "rich lady" underwear is La Perla, but in *reality* you're currently wearing five-year-old granny pants from Target. You'd probably freak out if I told you to get your dingy-ass to La Perla and splash out a couple of hundred bucks on a single set of frilly lingerie. That would just feel too scary or frivolous.

It could even cause you to spiral into your own personal brand of sabotage (more on that in the next chapter), and then you'd probably regret spending the money. Plus it would only be one pair of undies, so you'd still have to keep your old panties for the days when your special new ones were getting washed. That wouldn't make that much of a noticeable difference in your daily life. And honestly, it would just serve to highlight the massive contrast between your reality and the life you really want. One pair of panties wouldn't solve anything in the long term.

That's why, instead of making a massive leap that you don't feel ready for, I recommend going for a tiny, incremental upgrade. Choose the next best upgrade option from Target. Maybe you could upgrade to pretty sets from a mid-priced store and work your way from there up to the fanciest underwear, until you find your sweet spot. But wearing even *slightly* nicer panties will make you feel richer.

I'm not telling you where to shop: that's up to you to decide, based on what makes *you* feel rich. By the way, when I met Oprah Winfrey during her Australian tour, she asked me if I was wearing a Camilla caftan. I replied, "Of course! I wasn't going to wear Target to Oprah!"

Quick smart, she said, "Excuse me, dahling, it's *Tah-jay!* I wear Target flip flops all the time!"

So yeah, upgrade what's important to you. Even Oprah shops at Target and doesn't make it mean anything about herself!

Start with what will have the most impact on *your* daily life, rather than anyone else's. For me, that was workout clothes – because I lived in them (despite rarely going to the gym!) I threw out most of my old, worn-out leggings and sports bras, and just bought a couple of pieces from lululemon, even though the prices made me hyperventilate at first.

But gradually, I became accustomed to the quality, and they became my new normal. Every time I could afford to buy more, I threw out the old ones. Working out (or just plain *working* on my blog) just felt more abundant in lululemon, and I felt like a rich person. Soon it was an easy decision to only buy quality workout wear because I deserved it.

Now, nice undies might be easy for you – if so, don't choose that as your first upgrade. Pick something that really does bug you and makes you feel poor. It could be old makeup, scrappy towels full of holes, a broken chair in your kitchen, bad lighting in your bathroom, dirty windows in your office, or something else.

Choose what you'll upgrade first, then start from the bottom of the barrel and improve it as incrementally as you can handle right now.

Each time you upgrade something small, it becomes part of *who you are* and crowds out your old poverty story. It sends a clear message to the Universe that you're worth nice things, and that way you acclimatize to being richer.

This new way of being then becomes your new minimum standard, your "new normal"; and have you noticed that you always find money for things you value? The good feelings that this gives you on a daily basis compound over time, and the Universe provides the money for each upgrade because you're acting more congruently with your true inner self-worth. This isn't based on what you *say*, but on the action you actually take in your real world. The Universe rewards you when you reward yourself.

You're still tracking your income every day, right? As you continue to track that incoming money, you'll start to see that the Universe rewards you with actual *cash* for feeling richer. It always happens. When you start off incrementally, you'll get the urge to make bigger and better leaps as you feel braver and better about yourself. Track it and see.

You don't even need to spend that much money to feel richer. Sometimes the difference between the cheapest option and the next best is only a few bucks – especially for consumer goods like coffee or tea, chocolate, hummus, hand soap, or stockings. Your basic bar of cheap chocolate is a few dollars and the fancy version could be double that – but in the grand scheme of things, it's still a cheap luxury that will make you feel richer. Plus, you'll probably eat less of it!

Do you aspire to be a generous philanthropist, but think that it's way off in the future? Start being generous now. Why not donate your unwanted gift vouchers to others for an instant feel-good fix? Pay it forward and practice what it feels like to be a generously wealthy woman. It's an incremental upgrade that doesn't cost you anything.

Realize too that it's not the stingy money habits you need to give up: it's the *perception of yourself* that you have to shift. Change the perception that you're not the "kind of person" who chooses the fancy option, or stays in the nice hotel, or gets a cab instead of the bus.

Nobody is going to give you permission to be a wealthy woman. You have to create that reality by *feeling* it in small ways on a day-to-day basis. It's not enough to meditate or visualize being rich (although that's useful). Instead, you've got to put yourself *in* the reality by feeling it in the real world. You prove it to yourself through the small daily actions you take.

> "What you believe has more power
> than what you dream or wish or hope
> for. You become what you believe."
>
> Oprah Winfrey

3. Repeat, repeat, repeat

The upgrade process lasts forever – because your tastes and personal standards continue to change over time. Make a commitment to take everything to the next level, but remember that you don't have to do it all at once. Just pick one or two symbolic things to work on each week, and see how each one feels.

Challenge yourself to try out things that the "rich version" of you would do. Don't put any pressure on yourself to get it right the first time: either you'll like each upgrade, or it will help you to refine what's really important to you. Either way, it's going to be really useful information when you pay attention to the stories and beliefs that come up with each one.

For example, if you usually park miles away from your meetings, practice getting valet parking and see how it feels. That thirty bucks will teach you more about your money fears than reading fifty money books. It puts your new money beliefs to the test. It might uncover new stories (or old ones) that you need to release. It's *totally* okay to try something out and think *that's not for me*, but it's also okay to discover you love it so much that it becomes your new normal.

If you're a fast-food addict, you could try breaking your habit and upgrading the quality of your food. If you're already a whiz in the kitchen, take it to the next level and start buying better ingredients. Imagine the pleasure that cooking with real vanilla beans or fancy spices will give you. Or you might realize that you don't have expensive tastes after all, and that's okay too.

You could upgrade your beauty regime by going to the hair salon more frequently than you're used to. Maybe right now you wait until your dark (or grey) roots are practically down around your ears before you make an appointment. If so, go a little more regularly until you reach your sweet spot. Say yes to the extra hydration treatment. Get a blow-dry just for the hell of it.

I don't know about you but when I get a good blow-dry, I feel like a million bucks. The day feels sunnier, everyone smiles at me, and I'm practically bouncing down the street with my own personal wind machine, Beyoncé style. If that sounds like you too, that's the best fifty bucks you can spend to improve your money mindset. A lot of Lucky Bees have told me that upgrading their hair experience has been profound, as superficial as that sounds.

When I have a speaking engagement or a conference to attend, I'll always get my hair professionally blow-dried. It's just my new normal. Plus, you know how much time that saves me when I'm traveling? It's amazing, and it has a knock-on effect because I'm much more confident about talking to new people. It's a small price that I'm willing to pay for the luxurious feeling it gives me.

Looking and feeling great can have a direct impact on your earning potential too. It's a fact that well-groomed women earn more. Ignore the sexist undertones for a minute because the energy behind self-care actually does help. You'll attract better clients when you feel confident. Spending that money before it shows up is an awesome investment.

Make a highly symbolic upgrade

To really show the Universe you're serious about wanting more money in your life, you need to show how much you *value* money with highly symbolic upgrades.

One example for me was when I decided to get a bookkeeper. I'd been putting it off because I thought it was going to be expensive, and I felt like I shouldn't spend money on something like that. That was for more *established* business owners, not disorganized beginners like me.

What I realized was that if I wanted money to be a top priority in my life and in my business, I needed to be more organized with my money *now*, so I could become the "pro" I wanted to be. I was neglecting my bookkeeping, I never did my taxes on time, and I frequently had to pay late fines. Looking at my receipts piling up just made me want to vomit.

I had to find a symbolic upgrade that really told money: "Hey, you're a priority in my life," and showed the Universe that I was serious about going pro in my business.

I knew a bookkeeper was a great next step, but I didn't feel ready. I kept waiting for the money to show up before I showed up for my money. Every time I thought about my taxes or looked at my receipts piling up, I felt sick, ashamed, and unworthy.

It was a huge waste of energy, so I knew that this would be a symbolic upgrade for my finances. And when I finally decided to stop expending all that extra energy on doing something outside of my zone of genius, it was the best investment ever. Start as you mean to go on.

What do you need to upgrade in your business to go pro this year?

Think about the symbolic upgrades you can take that will show that you value money highly in your life.

You could start a business bank account, or get a better credit card that gives you reward points. You could get a separate business credit card. You could just pay your bills on time (or even early!) by setting up direct debits that go automatically out of your account. What are some of the things you're going to do now that really show money, "Hey, you and me, we're friends."?

Think about how it would feel if you prioritized money in your life – if you made wealth and affluence an absolute top priority in your life?

What would a millionaire choose?

Sarah, one of my Bootcampers, was going through a divorce and had to find a new place to live. She had looked at a variety of apartments: some cheap and some more expensive. She fell in love with a more expensive apartment, and knew she had to upgrade as a promise to her new life.

Sarah said, "At first, I wasn't exactly sure how I was going to pay for my new lifestyle, now I was divorced. But I remembered the lessons that Denise taught me, and after I made the commitment, things just kind of fell into place to make it happen."

Sarah had agonized over the decision of whether to take the more expensive apartment because she felt guilty about wanting an upgraded life. She even had friends tell her to get the cheaper one because it was the *sensible* thing to do. (Don't you hate that!?)

For Sarah, going for the more expensive place was symbolic of how she wanted her new life to be. She didn't want to just *settle*. And honestly, she really could afford the more expensive one – but she was still experiencing conflicting feelings about it.

"There was a kind of feeling of yes, that's the smart choice. That's the one that rationally I should probably go for because I would save some money. But I'd be in the same place in my life. It wouldn't really signify that anything was different. Whereas the new apartment totally signifies that my life is different," Sarah said.

When you're faced with a choice like this – where you have to decide whether to stay small and cheap or go big, bold, and expensive – ask yourself what the millionaire version of you would choose. Would you move into a one-bedroom condo, or the condo with two bedrooms and a study, so you can have a proper office and space to do your work? That way, with the extra space, you can show the Universe that you value your ability to make money.

You might be like Sarah and think, *I **shouldn't** want that!* It's like at some point you've been told you *shouldn't* want to have the best. You *shouldn't* want more. You *should* just be happy with what you've got or what you've been given (either by the Universe or by other people). Well, this whole book is about giving yourself permission to not only want better for yourself, but to upgrade your life in all the ways that are going to make it possible for your dreams to come true, no matter what they are.

This is not about being ostentatious, spending money unnecessarily, or becoming a person you don't want to be. This is about embracing your power and making your life better: enhancing who you are through money.

Practice being generous

A lot of women have a dream of becoming wealthy so they can give money away: a worthy ideal for sure. Some personal development and abundance teachers say you should tithe 10 percent of your income to charities, to your church, or to anywhere else that you get spiritual food. I think that's a beautiful practice; but again, don't get caught up in thinking that's the only way to get rich.

I love giving when I feel called to; and this past year, I made several large donations that pushed me right out of my comfort zone. Literally: I was sweating and feeling sick about it, but it also felt big and abundant and *exactly* in line with my vision of myself as a rich woman who is moved by something and gets out her checkbook to help.

It wasn't easy, but I had to step into that vision of myself and put up some cash. This is as true for the $100 donation I made in my first year of business, as it is for the multi-thousand dollar donations I make now. Both feel scary, so you have to work your way into that generosity *today* – not at some point in the future when you'll feel "richer."

So, if giving is important to you, start giving *now* in a way that makes you feel generous and happy. Experiment to find out what kind of philanthropist you'll be in the future. Start the process of *becoming* her now. If you give money to a homeless guy out of guilt, practice making a bigger contribution to a talented busker instead, and see how it feels. Read the newspapers, and when you see an inspiring story, send some money. It will feel much better than a regular direct debit to a charity that you never think about again.

Donate money to Kiva.org each month and see your contributions build up over time; or make a few big, splashy donations a few times a year.

Tip just a bit more than you're comfortable with, and practice feeling generous. That nervous feeling is good – it's training yourself to be more abundant *now*, not when you're richer tomorrow. Experiment and practice discernment with how you give your money *now*, and you'll start becoming that wealthy philanthropist today.

> *"The secret to living the life of your dreams is to start living the life of your dreams today, in every little way you possibly can."*
>
> MIKE DOOLEY

Making all these relatively minor upgrades before the big money shows up will show the Universe that you're ready for more, and that you really believe you deserve it. After a while, all the minor upgrading will add up to big leaps toward your ultimate goals.

Remember: you don't have to go on a crazy shopping spree, and I really don't recommend blowing out your credit card. That defeats the purpose of manifesting more money. Just start with one thing at a time, until it becomes part of your normal routine and you feel confident that you can always afford it. Then pick something else. Rinse and repeat.

> *"Whoever said money can't buy*
> *happiness didn't know where to shop."*
> GERTRUDE STEIN

Live like a wealthy person now

Live like a wealthy person before you're ready. Find ways to incorporate your dream life into your reality now. You'll honestly be surprised about how affordable it can be.

What does the wealthy version of you wear? Fancy or casual? You decide, but I really recommend that you start by decluttering your wardrobe and booking in to see a good stylist who'll help you to develop your own "wealthy women" style.

Hiring a stylist is an activity I always thought only rich women could afford. It's actually not that expensive; and in many big department stores, it's even free. It saves you time, money, and effort because you know the clothes they choose for you will look good, fit you well, and suit you.

That will save you so much money in the end, and you'll feel like a fancy, rich celebrity. You know how much fun it is to say to a friend: "Oh, this dress? My *stylist* picked it out for me!"? It's hilariously fun to practice feeling rich, and you don't have to be an asshole about it either. In fact, confide in your friend about how little it actually cost you, and expand *her* awareness of what's possible for her too.

This will have a huge impact on your manifesting ability – show the Universe that you're worth more, and you'll be rewarded for it.

You might think that you'll save money by buying a cheap pair of shoes. In the long run, though, you'll probably end up spending more because they just don't fit you right, and they won't make you feel fabulous. So you'll always be looking for that next pair.

Bootcamp member Claire chose to upgrade her clothes, and decided to buy the "expensive jeans" instead of her usual ones, even though a part of her didn't think she was the type of person to buy that brand.

"I just wear them over and over again, knowing they look amazing. It saves me even having to look in shops or worry about how they look, because I know they are perfect," Claire said.

What about outsourcing chores that you hate?

Mark and I are really busy people, and to be honest, cleaning is not our favorite thing to do. Okay, let me re-write that sentence with the truth: I'm a really lazy person, and I *hate* cleaning with a passion. I'm not that busy by design: I just don't want to spend my time cleaning. This isn't a new "rich

Denise" thing; I've always been this way. When my mum sent me to my room to clean, I'd sit against the door with a book and then clean everything in the last five minutes.

So years ago, even before we earned good money, Mark and I had a cleaner twice a month. We always knew that when we were rich – "one day" – we'd have a cleaner; however, knowing that we had to step into our dream life incrementally, we decided to try it out and get someone way before we could actually afford it.

And honestly, it's not like the extra money was just sitting there and we just reprioritized it from another big expenditure. We literally didn't have the money. That year, Mark and I decided that instead of giving each other expensive Christmas presents, we'd have a strict budget of $10 each.

Yet we had a cleaner, and I spent money on personal development courses. We decided that even though getting our cleaner felt like a big deal at the time, it was worth it because it made us feel rich in a way that presents didn't. And we loved it.

We were willing to sacrifice things we didn't care about in order to make an upgrade that would make us feel richer. We freed up time and energy to work on our careers and make even more money, so we always found the money *and* it paid off.

Then, when we moved into our penthouse – our first really First-Class living environment – we upgraded to a weekly cleaner, and the Universe tested our boundaries again. We interviewed some cleaners who didn't want to make beds or wash dishes or take out the garbage. *I don't want to be bossy and ask them to do things they don't want to do,* I found myself thinking.

Plus, having a weekly cleaner was bumping up against my old stories that rich people were lazy and exploitative. My mother cleaned houses when I was a kid – who was I to have a cleaner now?! I felt like a total bitch.

I knew that this most recent upgrade was just another test from the Universe. I decided to take back my power, and I was really clear and upfront about what I wanted in the interviews. I just said, "I totally respect that you don't want to do these things, but this is the job description. So no problem: it's not a good fit."

And of course, as soon as I gave myself permission to create my ideal life, we found a great cleaner who happily did everything we asked for. By being honest about my desires and not compromising, I ended up finding the perfect person.

When we started growing our family, we had to upgrade again – this time with a nanny/housekeeper to help with laundry, light tidying, and even meal preparation. We increased our cleaner's hours and added in more tasks, like changing the sheets and towels. We got more discerning about our wants. And I'm sure that as our family grows, we'll upgrade more. My dream is to have a full-time housekeeper, and maybe even a private chef (ooh, how decadent!)

But the point is, I had to start with that first hire – a cleaner twice a month. Each upgrade got me closer to the goal, gave me practice in managing someone, and avoided the sudden shock of hiring a full-time person.

Each upgrade is practice. Each upgrade helps you to become accustomed to your new life. It layers in your capacity to receive, and creates a really strong foundation for your First-Class life. You show the Universe that you're serious about *becoming* the person you've always wanted to be, and that you're not waiting for a windfall out of the sky.

Start today by imagining the life you want in the future, and taking just one practice step toward it.

Get ready for the money

Some upgrades will move faster than others. I told you how I manifested our penthouse, but how did I get ready for that with incremental upgrades? It didn't just happen overnight; and I didn't move house every six months to slightly bigger and better ones. This upgrade was actually a big leap in reality; and because I didn't want to move every six months, I had to upgrade my belief incrementally that it was actually even possible.

So I spent every weekend looking at beautiful houses on the internet. Then, when I felt braver, I went to auctions and open house days for increasingly expensive houses, to experience my ideal lifestyle – even just for a few minutes. Looking is free. I had to pretend that I believed I deserved to be there. After all, if you're afraid to even *pretend*, why would the Universe make it happen for you? You're clearly not ready yet.

"I belong here. This is my type of house. This is where I live," I affirmed every time I walked through those gorgeous homes. I pictured myself living there, and I whispered to myself, *Universe, this is what I want.*

My goal was cemented in the top of my mind whenever I visited these dream homes. I could see it, smell it, hear it, and, most importantly, *feel it*. And don't worry about feeling like a fraud – most real estate agents don't mind if you're just looking. They can tell the owner that they had more people through the house, and guess what – they'll get your business eventually!

I remember a few years ago, pretending to look at a million-dollar house. That estate agent was a bit snobby, but most were totally friendly. Guess who gets our business now? Walking through those houses when I couldn't afford it made way for me to believe that I could.

When I flew, and I was stuck in Economy Class right at the back of the plane, I'd imagine what it would be like to travel in First Class. I'd always make a point of pausing, as if I was about to move to the front of the plane. I worked on decluttering negative beliefs about traveling First Class – that it's a waste of money, or it's not worth it, etc.

Then I started upgrading incrementally – first by paying for a slightly better seat in Economy. (You'd be surprised how many people don't do this – so I usually got to sit in the very first row of Economy for less than fifty bucks.) Then I would use Frequent Flyer points to upgrade to Premium Economy. Then I actually *paid* for Premium Economy. Then I used points to upgrade to Business... and so on.

I couldn't go from Economy to Business straight away. I wasn't ready to invest that much. But I worked my way up to it. I acclimatized to Business Class until it felt like no big deal.

Practice makes perfect

Practice and try out the upgrades to see if you actually like them. I made one of my Money Bootcampers go and test-drive some cars to see what it would feel like to be able to drive the car of her dreams. She said that the expensive one felt meh, but the mid-priced one felt awesome.

Interesting information for her. She wasn't really looking for a new car, but she needed a breakthrough from her previous mindset of "we can't afford it, so we won't bother even looking." It doesn't sound like a big leap just to test-drive a car, but you might not know your real tastes and preferences until you try it out.

I'm also not a big fan of spending all of your money on just one outrageously expensive item at the cost of everything else. When Mark and I first lived together, we'd see people with tiny, cheap houses but the biggest flat-screen TV ever.

Personally, I think it's irresponsible to spend money you don't have on luxury goods, especially if the rest of your life is crap. That's why I love the incremental upgrade. You start with whatever is bugging you first, and just take it to the very next level. That way, you build your wealth mindset with a really solid foundation, and with few gaps on the way to being rich.

Until the money shows up, do whatever you can to get yourself closer to your First-Class life. Go and look at that super-expensive leather couch you've always wanted. Sit on it for a few minutes every week, and really feel what it would be like to have that beautiful piece of furniture in your home. You might love it, or you might realize that the leather gets sweaty or that it's not that comfortable. Good to know, right? But you'll learn to make decisions based on desire, not just on price.

Go into a nice department store and pretend you can buy anything in it – you're just choosing not to today. Ask questions about different items, try things on, and feel the difference. Learn to be discerning, and figure out what your taste actually would be if money weren't an issue. Decide exactly what color and style you'd have, based on your own preference instead of the price tag. As you visit parts of your dream life, put your hand on your heart and say to the Universe:

"IT'S MY TIME, AND I'M READY FOR MY FIRST-CLASS LIFE."

When I was an event planner in my twenties, I'd always go and look at the most expensive hotels and conference rooms – even if they were out of my client's budget – just to see what it felt like. I pretended that my colleague Phil was my personal assistant; maybe they saw right through me, but it helped me to feel more comfortable around luxury.

That's what these practice upgrades are about – increasing your capacity for pleasure, and helping you step into your life as a rich woman.

> *"It's that first step – getting out the door – that's the toughest. If you can do that, you've already won."*
> MARY J. BLIGE

The billionaire's phone

What kind of phone does a millionaire own? What about a billionaire? Maybe their phone is the same as yours: the latest iPhone or Galaxy. But it's probably not a cracked one, so if you're cheaping out in this area, it's time to upgrade. Of course, if you already have your version of a First-Class phone, you can pick something else.

There are some things that you'll upgrade to the point where you reach a natural limit, and then you'll choose to upgrade something else. Literally, if you had all the money in the world, you might still *choose* to have an iPhone. After all, buying the latest version isn't ridiculously expensive, unless you get a limited edition, gold-plated one.

Becoming a rich woman might not change some of your tastes, and you don't have to find new and inventive ways to spend more money just for the sake of it. You might still shop for food in the same way you do now: choosing organic produce and expensive tomatoes. So when you've reached the limit of your food upgrade, pick something else – there's no such thing as gold tomatoes (at least, I don't think so!)

First Class for you doesn't always have to mean the most expensive. Learn to feel good about spending money on things that bring you pleasure. Support local businesses, make ethical choices, and encourage others to do the same. Be generous with yourself first, and you'll become richer for it. Then you can create good in the world through your generosity too.

When you reach the pinnacle of what you'd probably choose if you were a billionaire, then pick something else to upgrade.

> *"Money won't buy happiness, unless we exchange it for the things that will bring happiness. If we don't know how to get any happiness out of five dollars, we won't know how to get it out of five hundred, or five thousand, or five hundred thousand."*
>
> ELEANOR H. PORTER

Being cheap with yourself

Most of us have to ease our way into feeling wealthy. You'll find your own natural standards over time and they'll become your new normal. Making the decision once to have a First-Class life saves so much energy.

It means you can stop agonizing over the small decisions – the ones that seem cheap, but cost you more in the long run. We sometimes make things difficult for ourselves because we're reluctant to pay the money for the right solution. Maybe we think we should do it ourselves; or deep down, we don't believe we deserve the very best.

An example of this in my own life happened when we had some gross puke stains on our carpet. I refuse to say who or what caused the stains, but I want to make it very clear that it wasn't me!

We tried to clean the stains ourselves, but they didn't totally come out; so they were still visible and a bit smelly. Every time I walked into the room, I could see them. They lingered in the back of my mind as one of those little annoyances that affected my daily life. None of which made me feel rich!

Finally, after three days of seething over those stains, I called a cleaning company who specialized in deep cleaning carpets. They came around with their giant machine; and in less than fifteen minutes they'd got all the stains out. It only cost $65.

Just sixty-five bucks to solve the problem – in fact, to *remove* the problem completely – and thus save me from looking at it or worrying about it ever again. But I have to admit, I was reluctant to pay the money: I thought that I should be able to do it myself, or that it was lazy to pay someone else to do it for us.

You might laugh, but female entrepreneurs are notorious for doing things that we should outsource to experts. Instead, we settle for the make-do fix. We feel like we "should" know how to do it alone. We not only polish the poop, we roll it in glitter for good measure!

Where in your life are you trying to polish a poop?

Maybe you try to do everything yourself, from websites to PR; or maybe you pay bits and pieces of money for cobbled-together solutions that don't quite work.

Maybe you're waiting to get the new laptop/iPad/iPhone because you can't yet justify the expense, or you don't feel ready for the best equipment. Do you know how many entrepreneurs are trying to create a million-dollar business on shitty equipment? It's just not going to work.

Maybe you're driving a car that is falling apart, and continuing to pay money to get it patched up instead of buying a new car. Or are you being loyal to a hairdresser or beauty therapist even if you aren't happy with their service anymore? Maybe you resent your partner because they buy new shoes and clothes when they need them, without feeling guilty about it. Men tend to do that!

The good news is that every time you choose the VIP or upgraded option – every time you choose to honor yourself, your time, and (let's face it) your mental health – the Universe rewards you.

Sometimes it's going to cost money to upgrade, and you just have to suck it up. Yes, upgrading might make you feel guilty and bring up all your money "stuff." But trust me, it will change the way you feel about yourself, and you'll attract more money to pay for it.

What are you going to do today to upgrade your life?

Pick one thing today in your day-to-day life that's wasting unnecessary energy, and immediately upgrade it – whether it costs money or not.

Call the cleaning company and book them in for a trial. Buy a few hours of the virtual assistant's time. Lock in the date for the new headshots by paying a small deposit. Go through your closet and chuck out everything that's not coming with you on the journey.

Sometimes, putting yourself in luxurious situations might feel uncomfortable. You might judge the people around you in the Jaguar showroom, or you might notice weird, rich-lady plastic surgery in the fancy tearoom. Remember: you can be the exact type of rich person you like.

The beautiful thing about an incremental upgrade is that you can take action on it straight away, and lack of money is no excuse.

Put your money where your mouth is

It's incredibly fun to find something new and symbolic to upgrade, but you have to take action before more money shows up in your life. It's *not* the other way around. You have to treat yourself as worthy *now*.

This is why I preach this important message: you don't have to win the lottery to achieve your dreams. There's nothing you can do to make that happen, except to buy a ticket and hope.

You're much better off making small upgrades in your everyday life – because you'll feel like you can control your success and take actions toward it. You can take a small action several times a day and *immediately* feel the change inside. Imagine if you bought a lottery ticket every hour or even every day. That would give you a gambling addiction and still wouldn't guarantee you a win.

But you have the power to create even more magic in your life through simple, everyday actions; and the Universe always rewards action. You'll see that new clients come in to help you pay for your travel. You'll see special deals so the upgrade won't cost as much as you feared. You'll be rewarded in thousands of small ways that will make it worth it. But you have to start *before* you're ready. Show the Universe that you're worth it *now*.

If you're experiencing resistance around something like this, it's not because the Universe is saying, "That's for everyone else and not for you!" Instead, the resistance is coming out because there's still something there you haven't cleared. Go back and declutter a belief or judgment that you have around money or rich people.

Remember: when in doubt, always go back to Step 1 of the Money Manifesting Formula.

Every upgrade action shows the Universe that you're worthy of living an abundant life. Because you are.

It's your time, and you're ready for the next step.

CHAPTER SUMMARY

❖ Don't wait until you're rich. You become rich by upgrading your life incrementally in ways that make you feel wealthy.

❖ Upgrading incrementally gives you a strong foundation to hold and retain your future wealth, so you don't sabotage it.

❖ Upgrade strategically by choosing the most symbolic Economy-Class things in your life. This will have the biggest impact on your manifesting ability.

❖ Practice feeling wealthy, so you can learn discernment and decide what's really important to you when you take price out of the equation.

❖ Rinse and repeat! You'll never run out of ways to upgrade your life.

Chapter 8

Dealing with Your Money Sabotages

"Each of us guards a gate of change that can only be unlocked from the inside."

MARILYN FERGUSON

*Y*ou have the best of intentions to change your life, and you're proud of yourself for embracing this new Lucky Bee lifestyle. You've been forgiving like a mofo, you've put a million positive reminders into your iPhone, and you're religiously tracking every single cent. You even picked up money in the street. I'm proud of you!

And then one day...

✦ You get a speeding fine or crash your car.

- You discover that you *owe* the taxman instead of getting the expected refund.
- Your relationship goes to shit.
- Your computer craps itself and dies.
- You suddenly go up two dress sizes.

What the hell is going on?!

Denise – you told me to forgive all the assholes in my past. I threw away all of my clothes, and bought some fancy-schmancy hand soap. I'm muttering my affirmations on the train like a crazy person. And now my life is falling apart? I'm going to burn this stupid book. Thanks for nothing.

Hold yer horses, pardner! It's just your sabotages talkin'.

Here's the good news, girlfriend. Get through this temporary wonky period, and you'll make a huge leap forward. *I promise.* It's just a test. Just your old zits coming up because you're cleaning everything out. I know it sucks, but it's the test before things improve.

Your sabotages are your default fear pattern showing up when things are going too well. It's that pesky feeling – like when you've stretched your elastic too far and you *ping* back into your old reality.

I have my own sabotaging behaviors, which I've worked hard to recognize and stop. Remember: you're always a work in progress, and more money doesn't mean that your life is going to be perfect.

When I was a kid, if something good happened, I was sure that something bad was about to follow it. Then, as an adult, I continued with this self-fulfilling mindset. Whenever anything good happened – like a new client, a promotion, or a cute guy asking me out – I'd feel good for about five seconds... and then I'd feel sick with anxiety. It was like I was waiting for the "piano to fall on my head." That's why so many bad things continued to happen to me: I totally manifested them!

When I was in my twenties, there was much less drama in my life than there had been in my childhood, but my body still kind of craved it in some way. So I created self-sabotaging behaviors. One thing I'd do was overeat until I felt sick. Or I'd get bored in my job and let things slip so I sabotaged my career. Or I went out with guys who were *all* wrong for me, and I stayed way too long in toxic friendships.

> *"There's an inherent thing in me where,*
> *if things are going too smooth, I'll*
> *sabotage the hell out of them, just to*
> *make the music more of a sanctuary."*
> DANIEL JOHNS OF SILVERCHAIR

Another sabotaging behavior I worked on in my business is perfectionism. Living by the "it has to be perfect or not at all" rule really cost me a lot over the years because I just wouldn't take action unless everything was exactly right.

For example, on some days it feels like a lot of hard work to put on makeup and do my hair when I have videos to make from home. Part of me says, *You can't appear in a video looking like crap. People will judge you!* So previously, I would *never* have made a video if I really didn't feel like getting "dressed up" that day.

Now, however, I just try to circumvent those self-sabotaging behaviors by asking myself, *What's the worst that could happen?* And of course we know what would

---

happen: nothing, because who cares?! So I push through that sabotaging behavior by just getting on with making those videos, even if they aren't perfect.

When you recognize your own signs of sabotage, you'll do it less and less. These days, perfectionism doesn't bother me that much. I'm much richer for it, and you will be too.

Your default sabotaging behaviors

Many women suffer from what I call RSI (Repetitive Sabotage Injury) because we're so predictable and we all have our own personal blend of sabotage that we repeat until we've learned the lesson.

Maybe you create more bills for yourself, e.g. speeding fines or parking fines, because you don't pay attention. Maybe you leave it too late to do your taxes, and so you get the inevitable fine. Maybe you know that your accountant isn't First Class, so you aren't getting all the deductions you really deserve.

I encourage my Lucky Bees to repeat the Money Bootcamp several times because each time, they find *new* ways of identifying their sabotaging patterns, and their different layers reveal themselves over time. The patterns show up in different and creative ways as they hit new income ceilings.

> *"I have a tendency to sabotage*
> *relationships and everything else*
> *in my life. Fear of success, fear of*
> *failure, fear of being afraid. Useless,*
> *good-for-nothing thoughts."*
> MICHAEL BUBLÉ

Why the hell do we do this?

Play around with your self-awareness to figure out why you're creating this drama in your life. Yes, it's hard to hear that you're creating the drama yourself – but you totally are, and it's not your fault.

I think the two quotes I've used above are really interesting because I've long suspected Daniel Johns and Michael Bublé of sabotaging their relationships. Daniel is the former front man of the 90s band Silverchair. He divorced fellow Australian Natalie Imbruglia, one of the most beautiful women in the world, and then suffered from anorexia and arthritis at the peak of his career, which prevented him from touring. Weirdly enough, one of our trips during the travel competition was to the couple's secret wedding venue in Queensland.

Singer Michael Bublé was engaged to the gorgeous actress Emily Blunt (he wrote his Grammy Award-nominated single *Everything* for her), but then he reportedly cheated on her. It's classic sabotage, and you'll see it again and again in successful people. They can't handle the success.

This form of self-sabotage seems to happen a lot in celebrity marriages. The sabotage happens when the celebrity doesn't believe deep down that they really deserve happiness as well as fame and money. It's all too much, so they sabotage it to feel more comfortable with what they think they really deserve.

Let's speculate for a moment...

Maybe you keep your life small to avoid upsetting somebody in it, or to stop yourself from getting too "big for your britches." Or perhaps...

✦ You fear the negative consequences of having a lot of money – because you unconsciously think something "bad" could happen to you.

✦ You don't want to piss people off.

✦ You don't want to draw attention to yourself.

✦ You don't want to have extra responsibility.

✦ You don't want to create more dramas in your life or jealousy from other people.

✦ It would be a drag to pay more taxes.

✦ Your brother/mother/best friend will get upset.

✦ People will think you're a bitch.

Are any of these hitting home? If so, don't worry: it's completely normal. These are some very common underlying reasons why women keep their lives stuck – and you're not alone.

Fear of saying no

It's really common for women to take responsibility for other people's financial situations. They assume responsibility for other people's lack of planning and money blocks; and often, they help others to manifest their goals at the expense of their own. If this is true for you, the possibility of having to refuse someone else's request for money can fill you with fear.

Saying no to requests around money is totally okay. You don't need to be responsible for others: it's *fine* to deny their requests for loans, discounts, or free business advice; and let them figure out for themselves how to make their dreams come true.

While doing my Bootcamp, Alana realized that she'd taken on the role of financial rescuer at the expense of her own goals, because she couldn't refuse to lend money to others.

"I always feel like I don't have enough money. But when I did the Hidden Treasure exercise during Bootcamp, I added up $25,000 that I'd lent to people; and I'd never asked for it back. I realized that this pattern came from my dad – it didn't matter how much he had, he was always willing to lend a hand to others," Alana said.

On the one hand it's a lovely, admirable quality to be so generous. On the other hand, that's a *lot* of money to not have in your own bank account when you're not living your own dreams. For Alana, it was an ingrained response to say yes to these requests without thinking, so we did some digging to see where the sabotage came from.

"I feel like I'm doing the right thing by helping out others; and that I'm being the good girl, and being responsible. I guess it comes from when I was growing up and my mother was sick (and I had to look after her). I've overextended my responsibility my entire life," Alana realized.

During Bootcamp, we workshopped ways that Alana could take back her power and begin to feel more comfortable with refusing to lend money. I asked Alana to role-play with a partner who'd ask her for money.

Even though it was just "pretend," she had trouble saying no at first. She felt terrible and guilty, but it became easier over time – and then she could say no to requests for money in her real life. It takes time to change old sabotaging behaviors and that's okay. You'll get there.

It might feel strange to practice these types of conversation, but the more you practice them, the more comfortable you'll be in real life when you have to say no. Have a friend or mastermind buddy play along with you.

> *"Friendship and money: oil and water."*
> MARIO PUZO

When these unwanted requests for money pop up, and you actually *do* have the money available, it's still okay to say no.

What are you afraid of? That the person will hate you, or call you a bitch? Or that you'll create even more drama in their life? What if you call and ask for loans to be paid back? *What are you afraid of?*

My mother had this situation recently: one of her friends was hinting that she needed a loan. This friend had *so* much money drama in her life because she constantly wasted it via a shopping addiction. My mother said, "Even if I gave her $100,000, it wouldn't help. It would be gone within weeks." Remember: money doesn't cure money blocks.

As usual, any kind of awkward money situation gives you incredible information to add to your forgiveness list. It will uncover new blocks and sabotages; and even when it feels hard, it's happening for a reason – so you can grow and change.

That's why it's so important to have a supportive community around you. The discussions we have daily in the Bootcamp are all about the hard lessons we're learning on the journey. You don't have to do this alone!

What's happening to me?

If you feel weird physically while you're reading this book, remember: it's just resistance and sabotage. It's totally normal to feel freaked out when you're growing and changing.

When you hit a new level of income resistance, don't hide away. Hitting resistance is a sign that it's time to go one step deeper, even deeper than before. You've most likely uncovered so many past experiences that your body is going through some serious changes and energetic shifts.

As you raise your energetic vibration around money, sometimes your physical body has to catch up. That can make you feel a little bit weird: out of sorts, out of body, or like you're just on another planet. Don't worry – it's completely normal to experience some "altitude sickness" on your way to the next level.

Just be gentle with yourself, and identify your sabotaging patterns without blaming yourself. Some sabotaging patterns are so common, and are just a normal rite of passage in life and business. I'll go through them for you below, so you can see that you're completely normal.

Pushing away success when you get "too" lucky

When you're manifesting like a mofo and you're winning all the time, it will get to a point when you think, *Is this too much? Can anyone really be this lucky?* It's exactly like in the Disney movie *Peter Pan*, when everyone is learning to fly by thinking happy thoughts. As soon as you let the doubt creep in, though, you start to fall.

I went through two years of winning everything I entered: scholarships, free courses, and famously, the six-month, all-expenses paid travel. Not surprisingly, I did start to get some negative feedback from other people that made me doubt my manifesting ability.

For example, my friends started saying "joking" things, like "I hate you – you're so lucky!" And well-meaning "concern trolls" asked, "Are you really sure it's sensible to leave your job to go traveling around the world – I mean, do you think you'll be able to get a proper job afterward?"

Let's not even go into what I was telling myself!

It started to freak me out a little bit; and I got to the point where I didn't want to tell anyone about my winnings, or the fact that I was super lucky. I felt embarrassed by my good fortune, and I stopped thinking happy thoughts.

That wasn't good for my manifesting mojo, so sure enough, I stopped winning so much. You need to be single-minded with your positive thoughts, so that anyone who tries to sidetrack you – consciously or unconsciously – won't be able to throw you off course.

Another example happened when I was at an event run by *Wildly Wealthy Fast* author Sandy Forster. I was chatting to the woman seated beside me, and I told her how I win everything, and that I wanted to win one of the lucky door prizes at the event. She was totally impressed with my track record of winning, but as soon as I told her, I started to feel sick about bragging so openly.

First I thought, *What if I win now? This woman is going to think I'm selfish for winning everything. Maybe I've won so much that I should just give other people a chance?*

Then I thought, *What if I don't win? I told her that I'm lucky and I win all the time, so she's going to think I'm a fraud.* All those little seeds of self-doubt crept into my mind.

Let me tell you, it's virtually impossible to consciously manifest success when you're freaking out. So, when the time came to draw the first prize, I knew that if I really did want to win, I had to push the negativity out of my mind and replace it with positive thoughts. I didn't want the Universe tuning into those negative fears, so I wrote on my piece of paper, "It's okay for me to win. It's okay for good things to happen to me all the time."

I sat with it, and I felt peace in my heart about the outcome. Either way, I would be safe. I did some EFT tapping on my hand under my table, saying to myself, *Even though I win all the time, I deeply and completely love and accept myself.*

As I was tapping away discreetly under my table, the winner was announced, and it was me! The woman next to me said, "Oh my God, you *do* win everything!"

When negative thoughts creep in, you just can't tune into them. Don't pay them any attention. They don't serve you, and they often stop you from manifesting what you want. I know it's hard, but I told you it was going to take 150 percent sometimes.

If you start to get dragged down by other people's reactions to your good fortune, just remember that your wealth is your responsibility alone. You can't get sidetracked from your journey by worrying about what other people think.

You can use the tools outlined in this book, like forgiveness and decluttering. You definitely need a pattern interrupter, so make sure you're wearing your elastic band, or that you practice your EFT. Ignore the naysayers, and make sure that you're surrounding yourself with an amazing community to remind you that you can do it.

> *"The only way not to think about
> money is to have a great deal of it."*
>
> EDITH WHARTON

You deserve the peace of mind that comes with being wealthy. You do deserve good things to happen to you – whether that means winning all the time or creating good outcomes. You do deserve to be lucky and live a First-Class life.

Giving up money responsibility

When I was twenty, I lived in a grungy student flat in Sydney. I was from a small town, so moving to the "Big City" was a big deal for me.

I lived with a few friends, including one who I'll call *Stacy*. I loved Stacy. She was the perfect slacker housemate. She rarely went to class, so some days we'd hang out playing card games and eating cheese on toast while watching *Friends* or *Bring it On*.

Stacy was responsible for paying our rent, which we did in cash back then. At the start of the month, we'd each give her $400 in cash, and she'd go to the bank to deposit it... old-school style. Only it turned out that she didn't always go *straight* to the bank. Sometimes she spent the money and replaced it days later – or not at all. But none of us knew that she was stealing our money.

About six months after Stacy took on this important responsibility, we got a call completely out of the blue from the landlord, telling us that we'd be evicted unless we coughed up thousands of dollars in unpaid rent. When we confronted Stacy, she admitted to what she'd done immediately, but I felt so betrayed. She was supposed to be my friend and she'd stolen from me. It sucked.

It was a harsh lesson, but you know what... I didn't really learn anything from it. In fact, I barely expressed my disappointment to her at all. She paid the money and moved out, but it wasn't my last harsh money lesson.

Over the next few years, I continued to give my money power away, and repeatedly ignored red flags around money. I could give you numerous examples – like getting into massive amounts of credit card debt or squandering money windfalls. I didn't even open my credit card statements for years.

There are many ways that women give away their power around money. Sometimes it takes a crisis to actually wake you up to it, while other times it's incredibly subtle.

One of my Bootcamp ladies, Jess, always paid for her friends when they went out for coffee or meals. It got to the point where her friends wouldn't even offer to pay anymore. They just waited until Jess reached for the check. She was getting resentful about it, but couldn't say anything because she felt like a bitch. Annoying, right?

During Bootcamp, Jess realized that this was an *old* pattern that went back to childhood, when she'd given away her pocket money to others. She'd felt bad and guilty that she earned more money than her friends, so she felt as though it was her responsibility to pay for them.

I suggested an assignment. Next time the restaurant check came, she had to sit and wait (on her hands if necessary). She couldn't be the first to make the move. She couldn't automatically offer to pay, even if it was excruciatingly awkward.

It was tough for her at first, but then she realized other things about her friends. They sat and bitched about money the whole time; and she went away from their get-togethers not only feeling resentful about their cheap-ass ways, but also deflated and depressed about money.

Bad feelings attract more bad feelings. That's why upgrading your network is so important; and honestly, a lot of women start to declutter their friendship groups when they commit to creating a First-Class life.

When Jess changed her standards, she started noticing these incongruities and how they made her feel. Her friends didn't change their behavior, but Jess changed her own. She had to transition to friendships with people who had the kind of relationship with money that she wanted.

I'm not saying that you need to ditch all your friends, but it's confronting when you realize how much other people's attitudes impact your money beliefs. Trust me: your relationships will start to shift – whether consciously or not – because the Universe has your best interests at heart.

The ostrich syndrome

Maybe your problem is not "over-responsibility," but rather denial. This was a big one of mine: I just thought that if I ignored a problem, it would go away.

Many of our Lucky Bees sabotage themselves through this "ostrich syndrome." For example, Beth realized that she wasn't taking any responsibility around money at all. Her husband paid for everything. She just put her income into a joint account, and let him organize all the bills.

She never opened a single one, until she found out later that they had thousands of dollars' worth of unexpected credit card debt. She blamed him, but she also had to take responsibility for her massive reluctance to see the problems herself.

Funnily enough, this too was an old family pattern. Beth's dad had left her mother with massive amounts of totally unexpected debt when he died.

Where are you giving up money responsibility to others in your life? Taking power back around your money is about getting the balance right. Taking either too much or too little responsibility holds you back from having a beautiful, healthy, and abundant relationship with your true wealthy self.

You don't need to get evicted, lose all your friends, or break up your marriage to learn the lesson. Take a look at where money is a pain in the butt for you, and ask yourself:

✦ Where has this shown up in my past?

✦ What's the pattern?

✦ What's the Universe trying to tell me?

✦ What am I afraid of?

✦ What am I no longer willing to put up with?

These simple but magical questions will uncover your go-to sabotage; and then once you figure out the lesson, you can clear it *forever*. Add anything you discover to your forgiveness list, and declutter the crap out of these memories, so you can stop repeating the pattern.

Groundhog Day: dealing with recurring problems

We really are creatures of habit, and our inner saboteurs aren't that creative. If you're not sure exactly how you're holding yourself back, look for recurring patterns in your life around money.

Be aware though that they aren't always easy to see. This is because you're just so *used* to them. They're just "how life is," or things you feel like you have no control over. Maybe they're all "someone else's fault."

It's like the friend who attracts the same bad boyfriend every time, and then wonders why it ends the exact same way as last time. What's the common denominator in the way money dramas come up in your life? *You!* (Sorry, honey. I know that's hard to hear.)

One of my Lucky Bees, Melissa, had a really annoying situation happen with a tradesman, which on the surface seemed like a one-off kind of thing. But after we peeled back a few layers, Melissa realized that she had repeatedly been bullied and ripped off by various people throughout her life; and that these repetitive episodes were holding her back from being truly wealthy.

She almost always paid more than she should, and felt resentful about it; and the work was often shoddy and cost her much more in the long run anyway. Of course, she justified it in perfectly rational-sounding ways:

◆ All tradesmen are dodgy anyway.

◆ These guys never know what they're doing.

◆ People will always try and rip you off.

◆ I should speak up: it's my fault.

✦ It's hard to find a good tradesman.

✦ I'm so unlucky with repairs!

Melissa realized that the situation with the dishwasher repairman was very similar to growing up with family who disrespected her, bullied her about her dreams, and often borrowed money without paying it back.

"At sixteen, I had a part-time job at the local shop. If my dad was short of cash, he'd always ask me to take my money out of my piggy bank and would never repay it," Melissa remembered. (By the way, this is a hugely common story – parents "stealing" your money and never repaying it.)

Melissa had an enormous sense of "this isn't *fair!*" But because she loved her dad, she never said anything to him. She felt powerless. Even though Melissa is a capable adult woman now, those memories still live within her; and they made her totally unconsciously decide something about the world:

✦ Life's not fair!

✦ Men rip me off.

✦ Nobody will take care of me.

✦ Everything will be taken from me.

✦ I have to give in or I'll get in trouble.

You might think I'm being overly dramatic, but I've seen the powerful financial transformation that women create when they eliminate *anything* from their past that affects their current self-esteem. Any of these little stories, even if they seem harmless, could be sabotaging your current relationship with money.

If something keeps showing up in your awareness, it's happening for a reason. It could show up as an annoying recurring situation, as obsessing about old arguments, or even as a dream. Regardless of the form, it's bringing your attention to something you should clear: either a memory from the past or a traumatic event that created a limiting self-belief.

Melissa wouldn't have felt safe being any wealthier than she was because it would have created even *more* situations where people who were supposed to love and take care of her, instead took advantage of her. She was sabotaging her financial situation to keep herself safe. Clearing those old memories of being powerless created space for more abundance in her life in a way that could make her feel powerful instead of bullied.

It's amazing when you figure out the lesson because you get an aha moment that illuminates your weird behavior or your "unluckiness" in a particular situation. Learn the lesson, and say to the Universe, "I get it. You can stop beating me over the head with it now." Honestly, say this – because the situation won't stop repeating until you learn the lesson. It's not because the Universe doesn't want to help you, so stop making up stories about the situations you're attracting.

Forgive all of the people involved, including yourself. Forgive yourself for allowing it to happen, or enabling it if you're responsible for any part of the situation. Forgive yourself for being a "coward," and letting others take away your power. Forgive your parents or ex-husband for taking your money. Forgive, forgive, forgive.

Give yourself permission to be rich without being ripped off, and without having to be bullied into giving it to others. Allow yourself to feel safe.

By doing some healing work like forgiveness, you'll be able to break the cycle of repeatedly creating the same situation. Learn the lesson and move on – just feel it lift off your shoulders, and leave it behind forever.

Limiting the wealth you're "really entitled to"

Many of my Bootcampers have great success in the beginning of the course, and then they'll inevitably hit a wall and feel like "it's too much." That's when the sabotage, backtracking, and doubt start to screw with your manifesting plans. You sabotage yourself by attracting unexpected bills, speeding fines, and unwanted debts; and money feels tighter than ever. You doubt that this manifesting stuff even works. You quit and give up.

If you're fighting with your partner right now over something really dumb, or spending money you don't have on things you don't need, I have news for you. It's not about the money at all!

Boom – you've just crashed into the boundary of your energetic income level. You've reached the limit of what you currently believe is possible.

Incidentally, the same thing often happens if you're going really well on your diet. You start to get more attention, you start to feel good about yourself... then it feels strangely weird. So you go to the fridge and eat a whole cake without knowing why. Anything to numb that fear.

As personal development author Gay Hendricks talks about in his amazing book *The Big Leap*, you've uncovered your own personal Upper Limit Problem. This problem is a "negative emotional reaction that occurs when anything positive enters our lives and leads to self-destructive behaviors. The Upper Limit Problem not only prevents happiness, but it actually stops us from achieving our goals."

This awesome book taught me more about my money sabotages than any other book about wealth. Because, as I mentioned above, it's usually not about the money at all. So, when something "bad" happens, don't convince yourself that you're not meant to lead a life of outrageous success and unbelievable wealth. Instead, remind yourself that you're just experiencing an Upper Limit Problem.

Note that just because you don't want a lot of money right now, it doesn't mean you necessarily have an Upper Limit Problem. We're not all motivated by big money goals or material things. You don't have to be a millionaire to live an amazing life.

Your energetic income level might be $5,000 right now, or it could be 1 million, or anything in between. And if you work on your money blocks using the tools in this book, your Upper Limit will be something completely different six months down the track. That's okay too.

The point is, it doesn't hurt to dream; plus it's okay to be as rich as you want. And that panic – that guilt – that comes up as you're doing this work... even hypothetically? That's valuable information to clear and declutter, so you can create more abundance in the real world.

Bootcamper Hannah was in a tight spot financially, and she and her husband had both said that they wouldn't "do anything big" in terms of gifts. But then her husband gave her a really amazing present at Christmas. Her immediate gut reaction was: "I really don't deserve this!" Instead of feeling good, the experience made her feel *horrible*.

When Hannah thought about it further, she realized that she didn't feel good about the gift because her past still lived with her. Her dad had abandoned her family and that experience made her believe at a really early age that she didn't deserve her father's love, money, protection, and care. So this seemingly innocent experience bumped up against what she thought was possible and what she was "allowed" to have.

And guess what she did? She added her parents to her forgiveness list, and forgave herself for not being "deserving" of gifts. Suddenly, she could receive without feeling bad about it, or further sabotaging herself. Sometimes you just need to remind yourself of old patterns and be aware of the stories you're telling yourself.

> *"It is not the man who has too little, but the man who craves more, that is poor."*
> SENECA

Memories of divorce and nasty fights over child support come up a lot for my Lucky Bees in Bootcamp. Many of them saw their parents bicker about the amount of child support the other parent "deserved"; and many women now use that memory as energetic "proof" that they're not worth it.

"When I look at women who I think have it all, I label them as a 'bitch'; and then I feel this mild repulsion toward them because they appear self-entitled and spoiled. It's everything my dad thought of my mum for wanting child support," says Lucky Bee Cassie.

When warring parents bring their own baggage to the conversation, the child often makes a decision about what they're "worth." They don't realize that one parent might have actually been trying to punish the other, using money as their weapon. Instead, the child wonders if there's something wrong with *them* that their dad (usually, but not always) doesn't want to pay money to support them. It's hugely damaging, and there's no wonder that the feelings of worthlessness carry into adulthood.

All children should be entitled to unconditional love and safety. When our parents hurt us at a very young age, it messes up our future energetic income *and* happiness levels. Then, when things feel "too good," it triggers all those old feelings of confusion and unworthiness.

If this section is triggering memories of your own parents' divorce, add all of these new realizations to your forgiveness list, and then clear them out of your life. The fights that your parents had about money decades ago shouldn't impact the amount of money you're allowed to have today. Let it go.

Old money stories you need to give up

When I did the Landmark Education Forum (a personal development course), I learned a powerful truth: humans like to make meaning out of everything. As Landmark says, "We are meaning-making machines."

The stories you're carrying from your past shape your current energetic income level. They're often the origin of most of your personal sabotages; and at worst, they play out repeatedly until you learn their lesson. It's annoying but true.

You know from learning about the Law of Attraction that strong emotion attracts results to you quickly; but only *you* have the power to choose whether you attract positivity or negativity. The Universe doesn't care: it will bring you what it thinks you're asking for. So, for example, if you're constantly living with the program of "I'm so broke," the Universe will create situations for you where you can justify being broke, hence the unexpected bills and money upsets.

You can choose to stop your sabotaging behavior in its tracks, however, and transform fear into power. You can even say out loud, "Hello old friend. I see you and I know what you're doing. Now f-off, please!"

Bootcamp member Becca had a customer who wanted a refund for a $1,000 dollar course, and it freaked her out. Now, refunds are a normal rite of passage in business, but many women take them personally. Immediately, Becca started worrying that if she *did* give this guy a refund, then all of a sudden, five other people would ask for their money back too. She started to doubt her ability as a coach. She started to worry herself sick that her course was too expensive, which then spiraled into her old self-defeating patterns:

✦ I'm not worth it.

✦ I don't deserve to be successful.

✦ There's something wrong with me.

✦ *Everyone's going to ask for their money back.*

If Becca had let her old sabotaging feelings escalate, she might have attracted a lot more refunds. Using the tools in this book, however, she stopped her train of thought dead in its tracks.

I also asked her, "What kind of gift is this guy giving you?" Because trust me, a situation like this is always a gift in disguise and an opportunity to break through to the next level of income. Whatever happens – whether it's a tax bill or a car that needs fixing – it's exactly the lesson you need to identify and eliminate your sabotage.

Once you've halted your default sabotaging behavior, you can also start to look at practical solutions. When she removed the "I'm not good enough!" story that her ego was trying to pull, Becca realized she had practical stuff that she needed to work on, nonjudgmentally. She needed to tighten up her refund policy, and put steps into place to ensure she attracted the right customers into her business in the first place.

Becca also looked at other potential solutions. Perhaps she could hire a customer service person to deal with refund inquiries. Maybe she could also create a refund procedure, instead of freaking out every time. And she could track her refund rates to ensure they were in line with industry averages, and only *then* look at why people were asking for their money back.

The key was that she made herself move out of fear mode and look objectively at both the situation and why she reacted the way she did. Once you do that, your sabotages lose their grip over you.

If Becca had stayed in panic mode, however, there would have been a lot of emotional charge attached to her situation. She could've made it really messy – not only by creating more refunds, but also by creating money drama in other areas of her life. Perhaps she could have manifested an unexpected tax bill, crashed her car, or picked a fight with her husband. By dropping the fear and choosing to look at it as a gift, though, she learned the lesson the Universe was trying to give her and moved on.

> *"Money is not the most important*
> *thing in the world. Love is.*
> *Fortunately, I love money."*
>
> JACKIE MASON

Believing you have to sacrifice to be rich

In my twenties, while I was experimenting with my career and businesses, a friend said to me, "You'd do anything for money, wouldn't you?" This came after I'd told her the hilarious (I thought) story of my taking part in a medical experiment and testing drugs for money.

My first thought was, *I didn't have a choice – I had to pay my university tuition. What a bitch!* I thought it was funny to tell the story about the medical experiment – how I was testing a morphine-based drug and had to will myself not to throw up, in case I got kicked out of the experiment. Yes, seriously. I got paid a few thousand bucks to lie around in a hospital bed and take morphine-based drugs (medically supervised, of course).

My friend was appalled that I would risk my health for money, but I was secretly proud of myself for "doing whatever it took" to earn the money to take care of myself when nobody else would. I didn't realize that this was my pattern and my own brand of sabotage. My underlying story was:

✦ I'm all alone.

✦ I have to take care of myself.

✦ Nobody loves me.

✦ I'm willing to do what it takes.

I literally couldn't see another way to earn the money, other than doing something other people weren't willing to do. I was proud of it!

When I extended that thinking to becoming rich, I had similar beliefs:

✦ You have to do unethical things to be rich.

✦ You have to work really hard.

✦ It's wrong to love money.

✦ It's going to be a painful road.

✦ I have to do it all by myself.

✦ I have to be willing to do what it takes.

You might *intellectually* think that you want to be rich, but your underlying story will create a conflicting self-fulfilling prophecy for you. It *will* be hard, lonely, and painful if you believe it will be.

You might believe that you'll have to sacrifice time with your family to be really successful, or that you'll need to skip going to the gym to put in more hours at the office to take your income to the next level. On the extreme end of things, you might believe that you'll lose all your friends, that your family will ask you for money, that you'll have to pay more taxes, that your children will get kidnapped for ransom, and lots of other bad things.

Yep – those latter ones all sound slightly ridiculous when you think about them *intellectually*. But if you have even a teeny tiny underlying fear around money, the Universe doesn't want to put you in danger, so you'll actively, unconsciously repel money from your life.

Not allowing it to be easy

Lucky Bee Candice felt like she couldn't have it all: a good marriage, money, *and* a great career. She felt like it was too much. Nobody can be that lucky, right? She also felt like she had to work hard *now*, so she could have a good time sometime later in life. But she couldn't enjoy it now.

"I used to get $50 allowance per week. When you're a young person, that's quite a lot of money," Candice said. The one thing my dad would always say to me was, 'Make sure you save it for later in life. Don't spend it all now.'

"I would sneak away and spend it. Even growing up through my teens, I would always spend money – because I was told not to. They also used to say, 'Make sure you stay in your full-time job and work till you're sixty-five.'"

This theme of "you can't have it all, so don't enjoy it now" kept recurring throughout Candice's life. So once she'd cleared that memory with forgiveness, she added an affirmation: "I deserve to enjoy life *now*. I'm worth spending money on *now*."

It doesn't matter whether you grew up rich or poor, seemingly inconsequential memories like this can totally affect how you deal with money as an adult. They'll also affect what you believe you have to sacrifice to be rich and happy.

> *"Money should not cost you your joy."*
> LAURENCE G. BOLDT

Even though we all have some sort of baggage from our past, your financial future can happen entirely on your own terms. Your ability to succeed and your future financial journey is negotiable – every single part of it.

When it's not safe to be powerful

Some of the women I see who are on the verge of success have been told throughout their life that their natural leadership ability or personal power is "wrong." Or they've been called bossy or bitchy.

This really pisses me off, especially when I think of some of the unethical and horrible rich people in the world. The gorgeous, smart, and creative women I know are the ones who *should* be rich – because they'd change the world for the better. They just needed to declutter their feelings around being powerful, and allow themselves to feel safe in showing up bigger in the world.

I hit a big issue with this in my second year of business, when I found it really hard to manage employees and contractors. I knew that to go past six figures, I couldn't do everything myself, but it *terrified* me to ask people for help.

So I experimented and hired a few people on a trial basis. It would go okay for a while, but then the person would unexpectedly rip me off, not do the work properly, or otherwise not work out. I once hired a woman but didn't give her any direction or tasks. I actually told her that she could work whatever hours she wanted. She never did the work, but I kept paying her... for twelve weeks. Talk about a boundaries problem!

Even after I found an amazing assistant, I shied away from asking her to do things for me. I felt bad; like I should do everything myself – even when my assistant was proactively asking to take tasks off my to-do list.

I still did my weekly newsletter when I was in hospital after my first baby, because I was resisting making my business easier for myself, even while on maternity leave.

I knew this was probably a recurring sabotage in my life, so I explored my past experiences around receiving help, accepting help, and being the leader I wanted to be. And bingo! It didn't take me long to figure it out.

There had been lots of times in my life where I got really negative feedback from taking charge. I used to start clubs with all my friends when I was about eight or nine. I was just a natural leader, so I wanted to be president of our "Cool Kids Club." (We had a club song and everything!) Sometimes the other kids would say, "You're so bossy, Denise!" That was probably before we knew the word "bitch," but that's kind of what they meant.

The same thing happened at school. I took on leadership roles, like organizing our end-of-year formal dance (prom) and being part of the fundraising committee or yearbook committee. I was even the dance captain of our performance group.

I was really organized and great at seeing what needed to be done, but I'd feel terrible if any of the other girls said anything slightly negative, like "Why does it have to be like that?" or "Who put you in charge?"

I had a massive fight with one girl over how to fold the table napkins at the prom. I was right (naturally), but all of these negative experiences made me think that being the leader was a bad thing, and I hadn't yet developed the leadership skills to be able to persuade or influence people.

At university, I joined AIESEC: an international student organization with lots of opportunities for leadership at a local, national, or international level. However, my experiences at high school had left me reluctant to step up and lead. I thought it was easier (and less painful!) to tag along with everyone else, but my natural leadership ability made people turn to me for answers.

Then the president of my local AIESEC chapter quit suddenly, and I was forced into the role because there was literally nobody else. I was extremely uncomfortable with telling people what to do. By that stage, I had better management skills, so I wasn't being bossy and bitchy; but the same emotions were surfacing, especially my familiar fear: "people will think I'm a bitch!" I had to fire one of my executive team members, and he actually *did* call me a bitch. It was horrible.

So, whenever I've had to step up, be the leader, and make decisions, I've always had these types of feelings. Even now, I sometimes have to remind myself that asking my assistant to help doesn't make me a bitch. But I'm *so* much better at it than I was before.

I've realized that all these past experiences meant I later made huge mistakes with virtually no boundaries in place. When I hired that woman I mentioned earlier, I basically left

congruent with your chosen price point. If you price too high because someone else told you to, you'll feel out of integrity. If you undercharge, then you'll often attract clients who don't value your service. But when you feel in complete alignment with your pricing, you'll naturally start to attract the right clients.

Choose Your New Price

Here's an easy intuition exercise you can try out today.

Sit down and ask yourself what you'd charge if you weren't scared. Take the first number that pops into your head; and then increase it gradually until you feel an internal *yes!*

It should feel exciting and a little bit scary.

In my second year of business, I hit a massive price ceiling and tried this exercise. At the time, my prices were $300 per session; and even though I'd started out at $75 and had increased every few months, I knew it was time to stretch myself again.

Demand for sessions was outstripping my available time, and I was confident in the results I was getting for my clients. I also knew that I wanted to be a premium brand, and wanted my prices to reflect that.

I asked myself what I should charge next: *Okay, what feels right? Is it $350, $450? How does $600 feel?* At one point I felt like puking, so I took it down a little bit and settled at

$550. The new price still felt like a stretch, but I'd reached my new pricing threshold.

Try it for yourself, or get a friend or your coach to ask you. Keep pushing yourself until you find your next price. (You can do this with income goals too.) It should feel like a stretch, but in an exciting way. Don't get caught up in the numbers I just shared. Start where *you* are right now, but push yourself to the next level.

The price you choose *has* to be congruent with your energy right now though; and that's why nobody else can set your prices but you. I once set a really big stretch income goal, but I could feel myself chickening out.

I realized that when I wrote out my goals, my income was different every time because I couldn't commit. Sometimes I wrote out my stretch goal, but other times there was a difference of $50,000 – or even a *$100,000*. From a Law of Attraction perspective, what message does that send to the Universe?

You are not the average of your industry

Here's another mistake that women make around pricing: they average out the prices of their competition. The same principle applies: don't base your prices on what other people in your industry think you should charge.

Why not? Because if you do, you're using *their* income Upper Limits as the basis for your own! You're taking on their money baggage! A lot of female entrepreneurs have massive resistance to earning money, so don't use your competition as your barometer.

It's okay to be the most expensive, and to challenge conventions about what's possible for your industry.

When I started out, most life coaches in my area charged $75–150 per session, so I started at the lower end of the market. I charged $75 per session, or $270 for a package of six sessions, making it $45 a session. I used everyone else's prices as the barometer for my own, making assumptions about their ability or client results.

When I started increasing my prices rapidly, I broke convention by being "expensive." This didn't feel comfortable because, honestly, it triggered other people. Like many women, I felt afraid to go outside the "crowd thinking" within my peer group. However, with all the money mindset work I was doing, I knew I needed to do it, even though it felt scary.

Yes, of course there's sometimes a limit to the price that the market will bear, but most women are way undercharging compared to what's truly possible.

You really can charge what you like if you're offering a service that people want – especially if you have an online business, because you can find clients all over the world. You can be a niche provider, which means you don't have to work with or be affordable for everyone. (I know that might push some of your buttons.)

Many women have resistance around charging premium pricing because they want to help everyone. But the paradox is that when you charge below your true value, you can only help a finite amount of people. When you take care of your own needs, and charge enough to create your version of a First-Class life, you have a lot more capacity to help others.

For example, you might have the time and creative energy to write a book like this one that makes your work affordable for more people. You can create group programs like my

Money Bootcamp to leverage your capacity to impact your community. You can create a lot of free resources and weekly articles for your audience. None of that happens by accident – it takes time and energy to be able to serve more people.

It's not unethical to charge more, especially if you know that you're great at what you do. A huge sign is that you're booked out, and physically can't take on any more clients.

One of my earliest coaches was really talented, but she was booked out months in advance because her prices were really low given the results she got for her clients. I told her I would pay double to be able to see her more regularly. Her response was that nobody would pay it. Well, for a start, I would have!

I actually stopped seeing her though – because I felt her money blocks were affecting our sessions, especially when she started criticizing my money goals. She just wasn't ready to charge more for many reasons, but her low prices probably affected her enjoyment of her work, and made her impatient and even resentful of other people's success.

You might think that nobody could afford your new prices, but don't make assumptions about what people can pay you. I've assumed people couldn't pay for coaching and then I found out that they'd bought a new car instead of investing in their business. Most of my wealthiest friends look like normal middle-class people.

One of my most successful girlfriends, Leonie Dawson, still dresses in tie-dyed hippie clothes and flip flops, and has perpetual bed-hair! Don't assume. Remember that old chestnut: when you assume, you make an ass out of u and me.

If you believe that you're surrounded by broke people, you'll only perpetuate that belief with your client base. If you believe energetically that you're too expensive, you'll hear that from your potential clients. It's not true, but you have to release the belief first before it can be reflected back to you.

By the way, some people will complain that you're too expensive, even if you just charge one dollar. And the flip side is – even if you were charging $10,000 for the exact same thing, there'll always be someone who thinks it's too cheap. It's weird but true.

Increase Your Capacity for More Income

What's your current capacity for wealth? You might think it's unlimited. *But is it really?* How do you know? Try this simple exercise to find out.

Write down your current income or business revenue. Now add 10 percent to the number and sit with it for a moment. How does it feel? Does it start to bump up against your own income Upper Limit?

Pay attention to any internal voices that come up and say things like this:

* Nope, that's not for you.

* You're not smart enough to earn that.

* Your clients will think you're a bitch.

* Nobody charges that much.

* Your industry contacts would think you're being demanding.

* You'll go broke and lose all your clients.

✤ That's too extreme: nobody would pay that much.

Okay – that's great information.

Now, what would happen if your prices or income increased by 20 percent? How does that feel? What if you doubled your income? How does that feel?

For some of you, this exercise might cause an immediate physical reaction. Your heart might start to pound, or you might get short of breath and start to freak out. Maybe it's really exciting to you!

Or you might think: *How the hell am I going to do that?*

It's not your job right now to figure that out, girlfriend. Your only job is to *dream it* and then clear any blocks that come up on your path to making more money.

Can you even remotely imagine that it's possible? After all, dreaming is free – and if "stuff" or resistance come up for you, then that's hugely valuable information to clear and release.

Remember: this is a lifelong process; and successfully raising your prices is not a one-time only thing. At some point you'll feel out of alignment again, and it'll be time to start the process from the beginning as you find new layers of the onion!

> *"Somebody said to me, 'But The Beatles were anti-materialistic.' That's a huge myth. John and I literally used to sit down and say, 'Now, let's write a swimming pool.'"*
>
> PAUL MCCARTNEY

No more bartering

Maybe you don't even have to raise your prices right now. Your biggest problem could be that you're not charging anything at all. And if so, you don't have a business: you have a hobby. This is especially important if you're dying to leave a job to make your business a full-time gig. I know it sounds obvious, but if you don't learn to accept money, you might be waiting a long time to make entrepreneurship a reality for you.

Giving away services for free seems to be a recurring theme with entrepreneurial women, and many get stuck at the bartering stage (where you exchange products or services with someone else). On the surface, bartering seems like a *fabulous* idea, especially when you have a low (or zero) budget to pay for services to grow your business.

But when you barter instead of getting paid for your work, you devalue yourself as a businesswoman. You also show the Universe that you don't see making money as a priority. It's a hugely symbolic decision to make, and I'm going to challenge you to create a "Zero Bartering" commitment as this month's inspired action.

I made this decision in my second year of business, and it changed my income dramatically. Suddenly the Universe was like, "She's finally in business!" and actual paying clients showed up rapidly.

In my first year of business, though, I bartered all the time. Mostly it was because I didn't want to say no, and have people think I was being a bitch. (Story of my life, right?!) At best, bartering energetically discounts your value. At worst, it takes you off-track in your business.

One of my first bartering arrangements was with a local photographer. We both had trouble charging appropriately for our services, so it seemed like a great idea to swap. I got amazing photographs out of it... and what did she get? I built her a website. *I'm not even a website developer.* I'd just built my own (shoddy and obviously amateur) blog, so I created an equally crap one for her. She totally got the raw end of that deal.

And that's usually the biggest problem with bartering. Not only does it energetically reaffirm that you're not really open for business, but one person often gets shafted. Think of your own experiences. Chances are that either you've bartered for something that you didn't really want because you didn't want to say no, or you didn't really get a great deal out of it.

Now, you might disagree with me here, and say that you've had *fabulous* experiences. Perhaps you would have worked together anyway, and the swap was of equal value, but it was just "easier" to barter instead of pay each other.

One of my money mentors, Kendall Summerhawk, said something that blew my mind: "It should never be inconvenient to swap money."

If you have equal services and truly value each other's work, then you should *literally* pay each other the money. Yes, you'll have to pay taxes on it and it will go through your books, but are you in business or not? You have to decide. I'm not going to judge you if you want to keep a small, cash-only business; but if you have a desire for more money and success, then start as you mean to go on.

So start your "Zero Bartering" commitment today. I guarantee that you'll receive a request in the next 24 hours, just as a test from the Universe. Just a simple "Thanks for the offer, but I don't barter my services anymore" is fine. Yes, you might feel like a bitch, but it will become easier every time you do it.

When you feel comfortable saying no, start denying requests for discounts too! You'll see a small amount of backlash, but most people will say, "Hey that's okay, no harm in asking!" That's right – no harm in asking, and no harm in saying no!

By doing this, you'll take back the power in your business and allow yourself to make great money. Not everyone will agree with you; but after all, it's *your* business, and you have the right to choose how you run it.

When you set a big income goal, you have to be energetically consistent and refuse to exchange your services with other people anymore. It gets to a point where you deserve to make *real* money for the work you do. It's part of being able to receive more; and it's a strong sign to the Universe that you're ready to be paid what you're worth.

When I had more resistance to making money, I'd get people asking if they could do my courses for free. Of course, it was just a test from the Universe, and that's exactly what will happen for you. You can even blame me, and say it's a part of your *Get Rich, Lucky Bitch* assignment!

As soon as you make the decision that you deserve to be paid, your income will increase. You'll have more opportunities to make more money, and you'll no longer align yourself to people who want freebies. If you want to give things away but still feel powerful around your money, organize a scholarship for your program or do a certain amount of *pro bono* work every year. But give yourself permission to make money from your talents.

Set boundaries on giving free advice

Megan, a Bootcamper who is a weight-loss coach, would get up to a couple of hundred emails *each day* with requests for help and advice. She used to spend hours answering each and every one with personalized advice and encouragement. A small percentage turned into actual paying clients, but most didn't – and why would they? They were essentially getting free consultations from her with no commitment on their part.

The endless back-and-forth of emails was eating up much of Megan's time and energy, without any payoff. Sometimes she didn't even get a thank you! Not surprisingly, she was far short of her income goals. Busy, yes. Wealthy? No.

Energetically, she didn't have a real business: she was an unpaid advice service. And although on the surface, it seemed like she was doing the nice, supportive thing, she was actually doing her clients a huge disservice.

Honestly, as much as you think that one email can change your client's life, what really helps them is the deep transformation that longer-term commitment can provide. Getting advice over email isn't going to keep them accountable, or pinpoint the deep blocks that they're facing every day. It's a very short-term solution; and frankly, it can be exhausting.

I challenged Megan to set boundaries and send a reply that simply said, "Thanks for your email. It sounds like you could do with some coaching to get the transformation you desire. Here's the link to my booking information."

Obviously, you can add more to that email, such as case studies or your business philosophy, so they can see whether you're a good fit for them. But make clear the next step they need to take to solve their problem. Maybe it's booking in for a free discovery session with you (after you pre-qualify them with a survey). Maybe it's buying your book. Eventually, you can even train your assistant to answer these on your behalf, which frees up your creative energy even more.

"While it was a scary step to make, it was actually very liberating!" Megan said. Setting boundaries can be a hugely confronting thing for women, especially if they have a block around receiving money for what they do.

You might even have a business philosophy that sounds good on the surface: "I don't care about money – I just want to help people!" While that sounds like a noble thought, guess what it prompts the Universe to send you? Lots of opportunities to help people for free!

Helping people and making money are *not* mutually exclusive. By being upfront in refusing requests for free help, you can save yourself huge amounts of time and energy, while still allowing yourself to keep caring for your community. You can send people to your valuable free information, like your blog, and then give them the opportunity for deeper transformation by working with you personally.

It doesn't mean that you don't care. People who are really serious about wanting your help won't mind paying for it; and it's a cleaner relationship when both parties have skin in the game.

Make a commitment from today that you're officially open for more business – and that means no more discounts, no more bargaining, and no more bartering. It might seem daunting, but this is the most symbolic inspired action you can take to start creating more money.

When you show the Universe that you believe your services are worth paying for, you'll start to attract more clients who believe that too, and are happy to pay you. Win-win for all.

> *"You are taking control of your money*
> *because doing so will make you feel*
> *happier and smarter, more confident,*
> *more content, and more useful."*
>
> JEAN CHATZKY

Overcoming income resistance

I'm going to repeat this for you – it's totally normal to feel resistance around increasing your prices. It's normal to have conflicting feelings around earning more money. No matter how many goals you set, and no matter how motivated or ambitious you are, don't blame yourself if you feel like you're bumping up against a new energetic income ceiling.

Don't be surprised when it happens again in the future either. It could come after a period where everything felt amazing and money flowed to you like crazy. It's normal, and it's part of growth as an entrepreneur with ambitious goals.

The good news is that you have everything you need in this book to break through it. The bad news is that eventually you'll hit the next ceiling. Sorry!

Every single time I raise my prices, it's really scary, *even now*. I worry that nobody will pay me – that someone will email saying "Who do you think you are, you *bitch*?" – and that my success will all go downhill. The difference is that nowadays, this feeling doesn't last too long, and I have the tools to get out of that funky place. You do too.

How often should you increase your prices?

Increase your prices as often as you like, but evaluate them at least every six months, to see if they still feel good to you. This just makes sure that your prices are still an energetic match, and that you're attracting your desired clients. At the *very minimum*, evaluate and increase your prices once a year, if only to keep up with the rate of inflation (and I know you can do better than that).

Honestly, though, there are no rules. You could raise your prices on your premium service every quarter if you want to. You might think that's too soon, but honestly, when you're doing this money block work, you'll energetically move very quickly – and the results you get for your clients will increase dramatically. It doesn't matter if you don't help people to make more money as part of your services – your new money mindset will spread throughout your business.

As you increase the prices on your most intensive work, you'll have more time to add other products and services for your community that don't require as much effort from you.

Look at your product funnel to ensure you have a mix of free or more affordable offerings (such as e-books, courses, or other non-1:1 products). This will make you feel really good about serving people who can't afford to work with you yet; *and* it means that you can keep your personal attention as a more premium-priced and exclusive offering. There are many places online where you can educate yourself around business models, and virtually every industry can add in opportunities to make passive income.

But it's okay to keep your personal time and attention for your more VIP clients. It's okay to be expensive. It's okay to be out of the budget of some people. You never want to be known as the cheapest in your industry. Undercutting everyone else is not a quick or fun way to become rich. Yes, it's going to press some buttons, but premium pricing is the way to go.

Whenever you hit old resistance, you might start to talk yourself out of everything on your goal list as "unrealistic" or "unnecessary." It's not unusual to do that, so don't worry. You'll probably downgrade your big income goal to something less scary, so you have the excuse to backtrack on your new prices.

You might even go back to old habits and buy economy items again, like cheap toilet paper or budget travel. You'll get a whole bunch of temptations – like old clients dropping out or people asking for loans. Recognize your pattern of RSI (Repetitive Sabotage Injury) and stay strong in everything you've learned so far. This is only a temporary test. This is a normal part of the process, and everyone goes through it.

"IT'S SAFE FOR ME TO BE RICH."

Imagine that you increase your prices this month, just by 10 percent. That's going to add up over the next year. What would you spend the extra money on? Travel? Peace of mind in paying your bills? Getting mortgage-free quicker? Donating more to charity? Making more upgrades to a First-Class life?

When you work on changing your money beliefs, it has a knock-on effect on the rest of your life. You might find yourself manifesting more than just money.

I asked Paula, one of my Money Bootcamp participants, what life is like for her now that she's regularly manifesting more money and working on her money blocks.

She said: "I feel so grateful. My life right now could be described as 'ask and it is given.' Two days ago I said to the Universe that I needed cash, and I found 250 euros out of the blue. I said to the Universe that I needed to buy organic olive oil because I'm running out of it, and my in-laws brought us a five-liter bottle from their trip.

"I said to the Universe that we needed to buy a vacuum cleaner for our new apartment, and we received an industrial Hoover that nobody uses anymore from my boyfriend's family. I said to the Universe that I needed a kitchen clock, and I found one in the box room.

"The list goes on and on and on... I'm waiting for the *huge* stuff to manifest now. I know for sure it's on the way! Thanks Universe, thanks Denise, and thanks Bootcamp!"

Life can *seriously* be that easy when you increase your energetic income level and allow yourself to receive.

> **"Money has no power other**
> **than that which we give it."**
> JIM STOVALL

How to become a good money saver

A really symbolic inspired action is to start a savings account or increase the amount you're saving. This sounds easy, but it might bring up some more stuff to declutter.

Have you ever got really gung ho about saving money and then had something unexpected come up that meant you had to "raid" your savings? Maybe you manifested something bad that wiped them out completely? Maybe you've told yourself that you're either a saver or a spender, and that you can never change.

A while ago, I realized a big connection to why I could never save money when I noticed that I was uncomfortable with having excess food around me. *What's the connection?* If there was food on my plate, I had to eat it all, even if I felt uncomfortable. It felt naughty and bad if there was even a scrap left, because of the "starving children in Africa." So I often over-ate as a form of body sabotage.

I realized that I was the *exact* same way with money. As I said earlier, I lived paycheck to paycheck, and if I had money in my purse, I had to consume (spend) it all. I didn't feel comfortable energetically unless I spent *every* single cent in my account by the end of the month. Even when I went shopping, I'd keep going until there was no money left, even if I had to spend my last $5 on a smoothie.

I felt guilty if I had more than I actually needed; so energetically, even if I saved money, I'd manifest an unexpected expense that put me back to square one again.

This is one of the most common blocks I see while working with women. They feel guilty if they have "spare" money lying around, and they feel like they should give it to others or consume it as quickly as possible. Trust me, this is *not* an income thing. I've seen the same behavior in women at all income levels.

I personally know people who easily blow through a million dollars a year because they are so uncomfortable with excess money that they do everything they can – consciously or not – to reduce it. It's like they're not allowed to have a comfortable buffer or to create an easy life.

Some women think that they'll become lazy if they don't have the adrenaline rush each month to hit their living expenses, or they try to "prove" to themselves that they can achieve any challenge, even self-imposed financial problems.

It almost doesn't matter how much you earn. If you have this block of being uncomfortable with excess (more than you "need") money, you'll find a way to spend it all. Even if you raise your prices, you might find a way to unconsciously increase your expenses – just enough that it doesn't make too much of a difference.

I had to train myself to get comfortable with having more money than I needed. Then magically, the same thing happened with my food. I became okay with saying "I'm done" and pushing it away. Whether it's with money or food, it's really healthy to start becoming okay with more abundance.

If you find it hard to save, see where else in your life you're uncomfortable with excess – whether it's pleasure, gifts, time, or anything else. If you're uncomfortable with having more than you need, it'll have a huge impact on your ability to save and make more money. Maybe you feel bad if someone gives you a present out of the blue, or if your husband buys you flowers "just because." Maybe you're a classic "re-gifter" because you think someone else deserves it more than you.

If you have this block, your action is to start a very small savings account and see what comes up for you. It might take some time for you to become accustomed to having a financial buffer – but trust me: you don't have to be perfect.

I've been saving money regularly for a while now, and it's amazing how different it feels. Instead of living on the brink financially, I live in a secure place of knowing that I'm taken care of if my income changes.

But this didn't happen overnight. Just like the concept of incremental upgrade, I started very small and got more comfortable with larger amounts. I literally started with saving $5 a week, and raided that savings account often. But it was an automatic direct debit, so it just started again the next week. I couldn't rely on doing it myself – because I would probably chicken out, or tell myself I couldn't afford it.

Even though I was earning good money and I kept raising my prices, I was weirdly scared to save it. It felt somehow "grown up," and I felt resentful that I wasn't "allowed" to spend it.

As usual, anything that triggers you is a great opportunity to clear and release old stories and blocks. I realized that I had a huge story about being irresponsible with money. As a kid, I often felt deprived, so whenever I had a bit of extra money, I went crazy and spent it quickly.

I didn't always think my purchases through when I was an adult either, because again, I didn't trust myself to spend it properly. I also felt like having money "just sitting around" was dangerous and wasteful when other people needed it more than me.

So I did forgiveness on myself for spending so excessively in the past – literally, I listed out all the "stupid" purchases I could remember – and tried this:

"IT'S SAFE FOR ME TO HAVE EXCESS MONEY."

Because that's what it felt like at first – it felt "excessive" to have money I didn't "use." When I realized that I never even missed the $5, I upped it to $7, then $15, then $22, then $33, then $50, and now I have a *very* healthy savings account that I don't feel tempted to spend at all.

At one point, I had a million dollars cash in my savings account for our dream house, and I'm sure I'll have that again (I'm pretty close to it right now – it's for another dream).

It still might not sound like a lot to start with five bucks, but I was so uncomfortable with the excess that I had never, ever in my life been able to save money.

Begin Saving Today

Set up an online savings account today, with a direct debit of a really small amount of money: one that you won't miss too much.

Every two months, increase it by another tiny amount.

See what comes up for you when you even think about it.

When you get comfortable having more money than you actually "need," you become wealthier, but you have to deal with this at an energetic level. That's when you turn excess into abundance – whether it's more money, more clients, more pleasure, or more anything else. That's how you create your First-Class life: you acclimatize to it, one step at a time.

The save-and-never-spend syndrome

Some women are the complete opposite, and are brilliant at saving money. But it's never enough to make them feel "safe" because they're so terrified of spending it and ending up poor. So they squirrel it away and never enjoy it. The extreme example is the little old lady who lived in poverty her whole life but gave millions away in her will.

If this sounds like you, examine why you don't like spending your money – because this will give you just as much valuable information. Is it because you think you don't deserve it? Are you worried that you'll be broke if you spend a little bit of the money? Maybe you're a reformed shopper who has swung toward the other extreme?

If it's not enough now, it will never be enough. You'll never feel safe enough, so you have to give yourself permission to feel good now.

Spend a Little for Pleasure

There's nothing wrong with having a huge amount of savings in the bank, but I'm going to encourage you to spend *some* of it.

Like the assignment for the "never savers," your action is about incremental spending, so you get used to actually spending your own money.

Take a small percentage of your income: say, 5 percent. Every month you *have* to spend that money on upgrades that bring you pleasure. Denise's orders!

Increase that amount over time, so you're spending at least 10 percent of your income on things that make you feel amazing.

This practice will totally change your life; instead of causing you to squander all your money like you fear, it will help you to manifest *even more* in your life.

Rearrange the Universe in your favor

> *"The world is more malleable than you think, and it's waiting for you to hammer it into shape."*
>
> BONO

Make a public commitment

When you're taking inspired action, one of the best things you can do is to make a public commitment, so you don't change your mind or chicken out. Here's the thing: when you've made a big announcement, either through your blog or newsletter (or some other public way), you're going to feel like it's real. If you're the only one who knows about your launch date, or the early bird deadline for your course, it's *really* easy to backtrack. Trust me: I've done it a million times.

This is why your inspired action has to be bold, and not just procrastination disguised as "busywork." Making big "real-world commitments" – being serious about them, but actually following through on your promise with real-world actions – will show the Universe that you're deadly serious about wanting to manifest more money. It shows that you're ready to take your life to the stratosphere of what's possible.

This is what separates the "rah rah" personal development junkies from the people who *actually* manifest amazing success in the real world. Positive thinking will only get you so far: now you also gotta hustle, girlfriend!

By the way, despite the title of this book, I don't necessarily believe in luck by itself: *except* when it comes to the well-known definition of "opportunity meeting preparation." I honestly believe that you make your own luck.

I really see success in life and business as being made up of hundreds of big commitments over time. Each one will feel big and scary, and you'll want to back out of it; but then, after you've achieved it, it'll be no big deal. That's why your commitments have to be things that stretch you, and they have to be public. Otherwise, the Universe just says, "Meh, she doesn't really mean it."

Remember the Pantene shampoo ad from the 1990s whose tagline was "It won't happen overnight, but it will happen"? Again, it's the same with getting rich. You have to regularly set realistic– but slightly scary – goals, so you can experience your wealth over *hundreds* of wins.

That's how you make it happen – not by winning the lottery. That way you won't become a millionaire overnight and then lose it all by buying a private jet or something stupid that you can't really afford.

Announce your new prices

As we've already discussed at length in the previous chapter, raising your prices is a huge, inspired action that will have an immediate impact on your income. And it's wonderful to say that you'll do it, but the best way to make the commitment stick is to make a public announcement, stating that your prices are going up, and when.

So that's your challenge today. Even if you haven't decided your exact price increase yet, put it on your website or newsletter, and figure out the details later. I've done this numerous times, by the way. I was too blocked to actually figure out a number, but I made a big announcement on my site: "My prices are going up at the end of the month, so make sure you book by then."

I didn't even say how much they were going to be, but I got more bookings than ever! And yes, I always finally figured out my new pricing by the end of the month. But if I hadn't made that public (and very imperfect) commitment, it would never have happened.

If you wait until you feel "ready," it will never happen, and you'll just be deluding yourself. The more public you make it, the less chance you'll back out. Yes, you might still have a momentary freak-out and get scared, but you can just push through. (Being scared is totally normal in business, by the way: it's not a sign that you're not going to make it.)

I'm a big fan of "fake it 'til you make it," and you'll be surprised how much other people take you at face value. People will believe you. The more people you tell about your new prices, the more their belief compounds; and then you just move forward automatically, without thinking about it.

This always astounds me. When I started writing books, I had to *force* myself to tell people I was an author. I didn't believe it; but the more I said it, the more I could see that other people believed me. People started asking me when my next book was coming out, and I was like, *Wow, they really think I'm a real writer!*

When you tell people your prices are going up, they'll believe you. When you say that your new course is launching on a particular date, they'll believe you. Because other people believe you, you'll start taking action toward it to make the deadline.

Taking action toward your goals, no matter how small, will help you to believe that it's possible. Just move forward "as if" it's happening. And before you know it, you've made a huge leap forward.

This doesn't just work for price increases, by the way. If your dream is to buy a house, go and see a mortgage broker or financial advisor to discuss financing. They will believe that you want to buy a house. (Why wouldn't they, after all?) They'll run the numbers and tell you how much you can borrow. Faced with that *real* number, you can go and tell a real estate agent that you're buying a house, and they'll believe you too! Go to open houses, and before long, you'll start to believe you're buying a house.

All these small actions will help you to act as if you're someone who's really buying a house. You'll start to tell your friends and family that you're buying a house; and they'll tell you their stories about when they bought a house, and they'll believe you too!

And then, before you know it, you'll actually be buying the house... but none of this will happen unless you make that series of small commitments. Instead, you'll be forever sitting in your old house by yourself with it all happening in your head. Get it out of your head and into the real world.

Remember: your inspired action can't be some vague, time-wasting action like "research." You can research pricing *forever*, but until you announce it, it's always going to be vague and theoretical.

So, go do it now. Even if you do a vague announcement on your social media pages – something like "Hey guys, my prices go up at the end of the month!" – that's a great start. You can figure out the rest later.

Pony up and put down some dollars

I love playing Texas Hold 'Em – especially for cash. I don't have to pay a lot of money to enjoy it. Even five bucks will keep me concentrated on my cards. But if I'm just playing "for fun," I'll bow out early, get distracted by TV or my phone, and take smaller risks. I literally have no investment in winning. You have to put some skin in the game, and that's the best commitment of all.

Another way to take an inspired action is to ensure that you've put your money where your mouth is. Don't wait for the money to show up before you commit. It works the other way around.

Put down that non-refundable deposit on the holiday, conference, or training course, and you'll move Heaven and

Earth to manifest the rest of the money. Wait until it falls from the sky before you commit, and you'll probably lose the chance.

I was talking to Lucky Bee Janelle, an awesome young entrepreneur who was frustrated about increasing her coaching prices. She told me that she was attracting time-wasters and people who tried to haggle with her all the time. She knew she wanted to price herself higher than her competition and her branding definitely reflected that – she was seriously talented, but something wasn't gelling. I asked her what was the most amount of money she'd ever spent on a course.

"About a hundred bucks, but I hardly ever spend money on courses,' she said. "I usually try to do a barter arrangement to get it free."

Um. Yep.

I lovingly pointed out that if she'd never experienced paying for a premium-priced course herself and had always bartered, chances are that she'd attract people with the exact same vibration. So even if you increase your prices all the time, you have to be congruent with your goal. You can't ask your clients to do something that you don't fundamentally believe in yourself. There's an energetic mismatch, and they *feel* it.

When I was seriously hustling in my business to go past six figures, I knew that I had to move house if I wanted to move to a bigger income level. We were living in a small, cute apartment, but it wasn't a millionaire's house. My office was the spare bedroom, which was supposed to house two single beds. To fit in my desk, we piled the beds on top of each other. So the back of my office chair touched this huge mound of mattresses.

Pretty hard to manifest a million-dollar business in that kind of space, right? Even though my clients couldn't see it, they could energetically feel it. It was a mismatch to my premium pricing.

So if you want to increase your prices, you often have to look at where you need to up the investment level in your own business. Going from a small apartment to a penthouse was just the action I needed to take to uplevel my life. Yours might be completely different, but you have to invest in yourself for the Universe to invest in *you*.

CHAPTER SUMMARY

❖ It's safe for you to earn more than other people in your life.

❖ Allow yourself to receive actual money, and say no to bartering.

❖ Income resistance is normal, but you'll break through each block – one at a time.

❖ Start saving and becoming comfortable with excess money.

❖ Fake it 'til you make it. The Universe can't tell the difference, and neither can your brain!

❖ Make sure you have some skin (i.e. money) in the game.

Chapter 10

Learn to Actually Receive Money

"Why you? Because there's no
one better. Why now?

Because tomorrow isn't soon enough."

DONNA BRAZILE

$\mathcal{S}$o, what's the final step of the Manifesting Formula? It's a really obvious one: you have to actually *receive* the money.

Okay, it might *seem* obvious – but it's not so easy for some women. In fact, when money starts to come into your life, you might fall back into old sabotaging patterns and resist it.

Go back to the birthday candle analogy we talked about earlier in this book. Around the same time that you learned never to share your wishes with others, you probably also learned that it was greedy to take more than your share. Don't be greedy, share with others if you have extra, and remember that it's more polite to refuse. Little girls, in particular, are praised for sharing, or for being a "good girl" because they give rather than receive.

And now that you're grown up, have you ever felt guilty for having good luck? Do you feel like someone else deserves it (whatever "it" is) more than you? And that you should help yourself last? This is incredibly common. You know the Bible quote "It is more blessed to give than to receive"? Many women unknowingly live by it.

Have you ever been out for dinner and wrestled a friend for the check because neither of you can receive the gift of a free meal? I have! But I've trained myself to say, "Thank you, that's so nice of you!" if it's my turn to receive.

If you're a parent, you've probably experienced this feeling too. The feeling that you'd rather your kids get everything *they* want, even if it means you miss out. Many women literally serve themselves last in their family, or eat their kids' leftovers, because they don't value themselves enough.

This is beautifully summed up by actress Teri Hatcher in her book *Burnt Toast*:

"Are you the kind of person who tries to scrape off the black? Do you throw it away, or do you just eat it? If you shrug and eat the toast, is it because you're willing to settle for less? Maybe you don't want to be wasteful, but if you go ahead and eat that blackened square of bread, then what you're really saying – to yourself and to the world – is that the piece of bread is worth more than your own satisfaction.

"Up 'til now, I ate the burnt toast."

Sometimes, you get so used to living like that, that when your fortune turns around, you don't know how to handle it. So don't worry if you've gotten to the end of this book and you *still* feel resistance to receiving money. You're breaking the habits of a lifetime.

Many women metaphorically and literally eat the burnt toast; but it's time for something else. It's your time and you *are* ready for the next step.

How do you know if you're resisting a gift from the Universe? Maybe you've thought things like:

◆ I'm not ready for that opportunity!

◆ Someone else deserves this more than me.

◆ I should give this to someone else.

◆ Maybe next year...

Or you find yourself procrastinating on doing something that will drive your life forward – like one Lucky Bee who procrastinated writing the book proposal that an agent had actually *asked* her for.

So, how do you really *receive* the money? It might take practice; and as usual, I recommend coming at it from all angles.

Maybe you need to *practically* receive the money. When I first self-published my books on Amazon, I didn't have the right tax information to actually receive my payments into my bank account. So I let the money build up in my Amazon account.

I was resisting receiving that money. Not only because it would cost me to do the paperwork (it ended up costing about $300), but because deep down, it felt like cheating to earn money on something that I'd already created.

I had to do something really practical to allow that money to flow to me. It sounds stupid to resist spending $300 to gain potentially thousands (I had around $1,500 built up in my account), but it's totally normal behavior.

At the start of my business, I always procrastinated on sending invoices because I felt bad asking people for the money. Now, as a successful business owner, I'm on the other side of it – chasing up suppliers so I can give them money! I know it's because they're probably second-guessing themselves and worrying whether they're worth it, while I just want to pay them the money!

What do *you* need to do to receive more money?

Some ideas:

❖ Sort out a tax situation.

❖ Transfer money from your PayPal account to your bank account.

❖ Ask for cash instead of a credit to your account.

❖ Do the paperwork.

❖ Apply for a new business structure.

❖ Set yourself up with a tax number.

❖ Send an invoice.

❖ Send a billing schedule.

❖ Literally throw away the burnt toast.

Or maybe you need to *emotionally* receive the money. This is where you need to go back to Step 1, Declutter, and give yourself permission to make money...

✦ Even if other people in your life are struggling.

✦ Even if you don't "work hard" for it.

✦ Even if you receive it for doing something "easy."

✦ Even though there are starving people in the world.

When you can reconcile the conflicting feelings, and allow yourself to receive money anyway, you'll get better and better at letting it flow to you. So revisit your forgiveness list and tap on any feelings as you identify them.

No need to be perfect

Step 5 of the Manifesting Formula is also about troubleshooting. As I said earlier, the Formula is designed as a circle – and when you get to the end, you'll probably need to go back to the beginning. Because (and I keep saying this!) there's always more to declutter. So…

✦ If you feel guilty when you make money, go back to
   Step 1: Declutter.

✦ If you're manifesting random stuff that's not quite what
   you wanted, go back to Step 2: Decide exactly what
   you want.

✦ If you're feeling doubtful about your goal ever coming
   true, revisit some of the positive anchoring exercises
   from Step 3: Surround your life with positivity.

✦ If you're feeling impatient, go back to Step 4: Take
   inspired action. There's always something you could be

doing in the limbo period between setting a goal and seeing it actually manifest.

✦ If you're having trouble receiving, well that's Step 5!

And so on. The work never stops: you just get quicker at doing the steps.

Trust me when I say that money doesn't solve money blocks. As I've told you repeatedly in this book, I still get blocked around money; and I don't know a single successful woman who's ever stopped working on herself.

But it will get easier. What used to stop me in my tracks for months at a time is often just a momentary thought now. I catch it, recognize the belief, do some EFT tapping, and then I can move on.

If you strive for progress, not perfection (which is impossible anyway), you'll gradually allow yourself to step into your First-Class life.

Anchor in your new money experience

In Neuro-linguistic Programming (NLP), anchoring simply means to deeply associate a good feeling with something else: to bring it into your subconscious so you can access it at will. In manifesting terms, this means you can return quickly to that positive feeling, so you can attract more goodness into your life.

I love celebrating and "anchoring in" successful experiences; and I believe that part of the reason my income has increased quickly is because I've celebrated every milestone. When you applaud yourself for every success, you anchor that experience into your subconscious, and you attract even more success.

Remember how, in my first month of business, I made $225? Even though I've heard other women berate themselves for being a failure for that kind of result, I celebrated it. I actually bought myself a bottle of champagne because I wanted to send a clear message to the Universe that I was proud of every single cent, and that I expected more was on its way.

Celebrating is a crucial part of receiving. It's a way of saying thank you to yourself – and to the Universe – for your good fortune.

Never stop learning and growing. But when amazing things happen, take a moment to anchor in the experience. Feel the *weight* of that experience, and don't be afraid to ask for more.

Lucky Bee Annalise said, "I realized that every time I got a new client or had a big win, I almost shuffled it under the carpet, so I could move on to whatever was next.

"When I started taking a few moments to anchor in the experience and celebrate it – sometimes with champagne, sometimes with just a pat on the back – I felt like I was layering in a more permanent foundation of success for my business. Plus it feels great to take a moment to remind myself of how far I've come!"

Many women are actually afraid to celebrate their achievements, for a few complex reasons:

+ They worry that if they acknowledge it, they'll jinx it.

+ They want to keep their success under the radar, so they won't attract something "bad" to balance it out.

- ✦ They feel guilty about it.
- ✦ They think it was a fluke, so it doesn't count.
- ✦ They try to minimize their involvement or work.
- ✦ They think that what they've achieved isn't good enough, so it doesn't count.
- ✦ They don't want to make other people feel bad about themselves.
- ✦ They don't want to be seen as bragging.

Is it any wonder that we women have trouble receiving?

I've deliberately created space in the Bootcamp forum for women to "brag" and celebrate without fear. I've banned disclaimers such as "I know it's not as big as other people's here, but I want to celebrate..." or "It's probably a fluke, but....".

You've gotta cut that shit out and learn to receive graciously from the Universe, knowing that you 100 percent deserve it.

So celebrate your money wins (I used to text Mark every single time I got a new client), celebrate your testimonials, and give yourself a pat on the back every time you experience one of those scary rites of passage – like your first hater or your first refund request.

Other people will see those things as evidence that they aren't meant to be successful, but you'll see them as important stages on your way to your First-Class life.

Make sure you have safe places around you to brag. Not everyone will be supportive of you, and that's okay. Consider joining us in the Bootcamp if you need to uplevel the support you receive from the people around you.

Here's what Lucky Bee Stacey Harris said about the support she receives there: "The community of Lucky Bitches is *powerful*. The support you get around the content, and the energy of the community, is so amazing. You can go for support, you can go for accountability, and you have a place to go to celebrate without judgment."

I'm sending over my sincerest congratulations and acknowledgment, right now, for everything you're doing in your life. I know you're working hard to create an incredible life for yourself. Plus, if you're breaking massive poverty cycles in your family, *never* underestimate how difficult that is. You're doing an amazing job that will impact generations to come.

CHAPTER SUMMARY

❖ Get practical and set up systems, so you can easily receive money and make it easy for clients to pay you.

❖ Give yourself energetic permission to make money, and revisit the decluttering exercises in Chapter 4 if you feel resistance.

❖ Anchor in every money win – big and small – so you can compound all of the good feelings and attract more.

❖ You don't have to be perfect – this is a lifelong process. Dust yourself off, and try again. It's worth it – *you are* worth it.

Conclusion

Final Thoughts – From Zero to Millionaire

*O*ne thing I've learned over my abundance journey is that making money gets easier and easier. You'll discover this for yourself as you get richer.

Success breeds more success

They say that in business, making your first million is the hardest. But for me, the first $1,000 felt pretty hard – because I was fighting against my money blocks the whole time. I never gave up the belief that I was meant to be rich though. Breaking past the $100k-mark felt hard because I had to change my perception of myself to "someone who was a six-figure earner." But honestly, after that, the ride to a million wasn't too hard.

If you don't have cheerleaders in your life, though, you have to do it for yourself. What's the alternative – that you never get to live your dream life? No way.

So be completely biased toward yourself. Become a relentless optimist; and see everything as evidence that you're totally on track.

The more evidence you collect that you're successful, the easier it will be to attract more of the same. Over the next couple of days, I'd love you to commit to celebrating the successes that you've been able to bring into your life through the changes you've made around money.

See how far you've come in dealing with negative people or situations in your life – and how much stronger you are. Celebrate the new boundaries. Total up every single cent of extra money or free things that you've brought in from reading this book; and congratulate yourself on your new energetic income. You've done that all by yourself.

You might not buy a bottle of champagne every time you achieve a new goal – but it's always worth taking a moment to acknowledge yourself.

I get messages every day from women all around the world saying that I've changed their lives. While that's nice for my ego, I always respond with: "Congratulations, you've done the work!"

Say to yourself, "I'm really proud of you, babe. Well done!"

I'm proud of you too.

Be rich, don't try to get rich

As you've read, it's not about *trying* to get rich. It's about being rich *now*. Don't try get-rich-quick schemes. Honestly, they never work.

What *does* work is to consistently and clearly tell the Universe exactly what you want, and then show it that you mean business. I really hope that you use the information in this book to create amazing things in the world with your new wealthy mindset. It starts with the decision that you *already are rich*.

It really can be that easy.

You are exactly where you need to be

If you feel like you haven't achieved everything that you wanted to by this stage in your life, don't worry. You're exactly where you need to be right now, and you found this book for a reason. It's actually the perfect time – because there's never been an opportunity like today.

You might feel like you should be doing things quicker: doing more forgiveness work, manifesting more money, and getting further along in your journey.

The problem is that when you allow yourself to feel like that, you're *always* going to feel like that. You're always going to feel like you're a step behind if your underlying message to yourself is "I'm not enough." Constant clearing, through life-changing tools like forgiveness and EFT, will help you to deal with those feelings. I use them every single day – so stop looking for advanced strategies and just repeat the basics.

Put your hand on your heart and say out loud:

**"I'M EXACTLY WHERE I'M SUPPOSED
TO BE. IT'S MY TIME, AND I'M
READY FOR THE NEXT STEP."**

You're never going back

It's easy to get excited when you learn a new personal development tool, or discover a new author. Once the hype wears off, though, you're exactly the same as before.

That's pretty normal, and I've been there many times in my own life. The difference now is that I've given myself permission to be imperfect. It's a simple mindset shift: just give yourself permission to start again. As long as you have your commitment to create a First-Class life, it doesn't matter how many times you have to remind yourself.

Falling off the wagon is completely normal. Just dust yourself off and try again. There's a great ancient Japanese saying: "Fall down seven times, stand up eight." And trust me, this should be the motto of *all* entrepreneurs. Go back to the start, and get back on track.

Let's make a commitment together that this is a permanent change for you, and that you're never going back to how you used to be with money. Never.

It's okay to love money, because money loves you!

No matter what, I want you to know that the Universe does love you, and money just wants to take care of you. You're allowed to have a First-Class life. It's allowed to be easy and carefree.

It's okay to love money. It's okay to talk about it, to invite it to play with you, and to enjoy spending it. You aren't alone. There are hundreds of thousands (and I hope one day, *millions*) of women like you who are embracing the Lucky Bee way of life. Just by reading this book, you've joined a global network of Lucky Bees. Together we're changing the way we each think about money. Together we're changing the world.

> *"I want to enjoy money. I want to like*
> *money. I want to like having money.*
> *I want to like touching money. I want*
> *to like getting money and spending*
> *it. I want to feel good about money. I*
> *want to have more money than I know*
> *how to spend. I want to be able to feel*
> *exhilarated when I think of money."*
> BERNADETTE WULF

You can choose your own adventure

Never forget: your future is entirely up to you. There are many different financial realities that you could choose; and there are so many different possibilities for your life, each one just as real as the next.

Imagine that each of these future possibilities is an individual bubble. Each one contains a different version of you. Rich, poor, or every shade in between. You can choose which path and which journey you take in this lifetime. Just choose the bubble that looks the most appealing, and step into it! You have the power, and there's never been a better time than now. As the saying goes, "If not now, then when? If not you, then who?"

I promise that if you follow just some of the lessons in this book, you'll become richer in spirit *and* in your bank account.

Your First-Class life is out there, waiting for you; and by making all those little upgrades and becoming the VIP you were born to be, you'll get closer to it every day.

In fact, just by reading this book, you've begun your financial makeover. Yes, sometimes it won't be an easy ride; and of course your path will have ups and downs. But believe that your success is inevitable and it will be, you Lucky Bee!

This isn't the end

Today is your lucky day! You don't have to wait. You can literally choose to step into your First-Class life now. And I'm always here to help you.

It was sooo hard to come to this final chapter! This book felt like it would never end: not because of (too much) procrastination on my part, but because there was so much I wanted to share with you about creating amazing abundance in your life. OMG, can't we just hang out together forever?

Do you know how few people actually finish most books? Even on my courses, only a small percentage of people actually follow through to the end. So congrats for getting here, and thank you.

I sincerely hope that reading this book has inspired you to start making some big changes in your life, and in the way you deal with your money. Re-read the book when you need an extra injection of Lucky Bee energy, highlight the parts you really need to learn, and give yourself permission to grow and change.

I know you're well on your transformational journey to becoming a wealthy woman. But this isn't the end. I'd love to invite you to join our global community of women who are changing the world by embracing outrageous success, and claiming the title of "Lucky Bee."

Make sure you follow me on all the various social accounts, and tag me in your book pictures (it seriously makes my day); and if you want to deepen our new friendship, come and join us in Money Bootcamp.

I wish you all the luck, love, and abundance in the world. You're worth it.

xx Denise